The Complete Guide

to

Book
Marketing

THE
Complete Guide
to
Book
Marketing

DAVID COLE

Revised Edition

ALLWORTH PRESS
NEW YORK

08 07 06 05 04 03   5 4 3 2 1

Published by Allworth Press
An imprint of Allworth Communications
10 East 23rd Street, New York, NY 10010

Cover design by Derek Bacchus

Page composition/typography by SR Desktop Services, Ridge, NY

ISBN: 1-58115-322-8

Library of Congress Catalog Card Number: 98-74530

Printed in Canada

To Mary Lee and Aaron

Contents

    Informed Strategies
    Publishers and Authors Working Together

    The Difference Between Sales and Marketing
    Maximizing Revenues
    Making Your Efforts Cost-Effective
    Calculating the Financial Parameters
    A Model Profitability Analysis
    How Much Should You Spend?
    Put Your Marketing Plan on Paper
    Start Marketing Now
    Marketing Timeline

    Create a Package That Attracts Buyers
    Know the Competition
    Publish for the Frontlist and the Backlist
    Advertise Only When Appropriate
    Build and Market a Publishing Identity
    Brand Your Company, Imprint, or Series
    Partner with Nonpublishing Organizations

Acknowledgments

I would particularly like to thank the following people who contributed to this work by generously sharing information and expertise: Robin Bartlett, Karen Bouris, Patti Breitman, Nenelle Bunnin, Paddy Calistro, Ani Chamichian, Philip Curson, Dan Dixon, Simon Fillat, Lenny Friedman, Peter Goodman, John Gould, Peter Handel, Grady Hesters, John Hunt, Michael Kazan, Brenda Knight, Debra Lande, Nina Lesowitz, Jerry Marino, Marjorie McAneny, Jennie McDonald, Kirsty Melville, Munro Magruder, Michael Morgan, Jan Nathan, Matthew Osborn, C. D. Payne, Gary-Paul Prince, Barbara Ras, Susan Reich, Brian Romer, Larry Rood, Carla Ruff, Claudia Schaab, John Sharp, Laura Simonds, Alan Shrader, Neil Torres, Maureen Watts, Skye Wentworth, and Tom White.

I would also like to express my appreciation to publishing colleagues from whom I have learned a great deal over the years and whose insights have contributed to my approach: Pat Anderson, Will Glennon, Lloyd Kahn, Lee Langhammer Law, Malcolm Margolin, the late Sebastian Orfali, Steve Piersanti, Mary Jane Ryan, Steven Scholl, Barbara Stevenson, Jake Warner, and many more. My apologies to all whose names I have inadvertently omitted.

I want to thank Jim Sinkinson, publisher of *Bulldog Reporter's Book Marketing and Publicity* newsletter, as well as editors Jesse Fahnestock, Judy Hirni, and Rob Nylund. Some of this material first appeared in that newsletter in slightly different form.

Two articles I wrote for the PMA Newsletter, "Eight Rules for Effective Marketing Copy" and "Strengthen Backlist Sales and Your Profits," have also been adapted for use in this book.

Special thanks to several people who have allowed me to use materials in this book: Patsy Barich for the *Entrepreneurial Couples* press kit; Kathi Kamen Goldmark for her "Tips to Authors for Effective Bookstore Appearances;" and Maureen Watts for the *Stretch-ware*, *Red Wine for Dummies*™, and *Wine for Dummies*™, Second Edition, press releases.

Preface to the
Second Edition

Throughout the last century, as each new communication and entertainment technology emerged—movies, radio, television, computers, CD-ROMs, and the Internet—cultural commentators and business skeptics have predicted the demise of books. Nevertheless, the industry has grown and thrived—although sometimes more slowly than competing industries—and it continues to grow in real terms. With U.S. sales of more than $26 billion in 2002, book publishing has expanded (with the numbers adjusted for inflation) at a rate of 2 to 4 percent a year over the past ten years. (Total U.S. sales in 1992 were $17 billion.)

Even as these numbers suggest a slow-moving, if not stagnant, industry, profound changes have taken place during the last decade that have affected dominant players and smaller businesses alike. These changes are in many ways parallel to changes in other industries and are most noticeable in the consolidation of retail chains and publishing giants, and in the just-in-time inventory practices, which are rooted in new IT capacities, production efficiency, and the availability of overnight shipping.

Currently about 60,000 books are published each year in the United States, and while it is estimated that there are 30,000 publishers active in the nation, the vast majority of sales are made by a few international corporations that have grown immensely in the last decade through mergers and acquisitions. These include the German-based Bertelsmann (owner in the United States of Random House, Bantam, Doubleday, Dell, and all major book clubs), the U.K.-based Pearson (owner of Penguin, Putnam, Prentice-Hall, Scott-Foresman, etc.), the U.K.-based Collins (owner in the United States of HarperCollins) as well as U.S.-based corporations with international businesses such as McGraw-Hill, Viacom (owner of Simon & Schuster), and Time Warner.

In a parallel development, large chain bookstores and online retailers dominate the retail marketplace. Currently, the large chain bookstores (Barnes & Noble and Borders) account for about 25 percent of the trade market, with small chains and independent booksellers accounting for about 15 percent. Two other channels that have experienced explosive growth in the last few years, warehouse clubs and online sales, now account for between 6 and 7 percent of the market. The remaining trade book sales are divided among book clubs, discounters, mail-order businesses, mass merchandisers, groceries and drugstores, and used bookstores.

The net impact of all of these changes has been to increase competition while narrowing margins for publishers, wholesalers, distributors, and bookstores. This, of course, means that all involved are constantly looking for ways to increase sales volume. While price increases often provide the solution in such situations, for the publishing industry this is possible only to a small degree since books are competing against other forms of entertainment and sources of information, and consumer resistance to higher priced books is formidable. In summary, publishers, bookstores, and middlemen are increasingly looking to blockbuster bestsellers for their profits.

In the midst of a seemingly unstoppable trend toward agglomeration and globalization, small and medium-size publishers have identified and profited from the countervailing desire of consumers for a greater variety in what they buy and read. Similar to the trend in consumer magazines where broad-based consumer stalwarts—*Life, Look, Time,* and *Newsweek,* for instance—have been displaced by a plethora of specialized titles appealing to a narrowly segmented audience, niche publishers have found that they must specialize to survive. They can't compete for the largest markets with the big corporations, but they can profit by serving small audiences well.

In this light, I think the advice in this book has grown more valuable. In updating the text, I have added a number of sidebars with practical examples from publishers in different portions of the industry, from small independent and university presses to divisions of corporate players. I have deleted some material where markets have changed and rewritten whole sections where conditions have changed significantly.

Introduction:
Marketing Is Everything—
Everything Is Marketing

As diverse and unpredictable as the world in which we live, the book publishing industry in recent years has been affected by all the changes and pressures that have taken place around us, and paradoxes abound. Despite the contribution of technology toward more efficient and lower production costs, margins have narrowed. While the number of titles on bookstore shelves has greatly increased because of superstores, competition for the attention of consumers has increased proportionately. Though overall sales figures continue to grow, the sales volume required to make a book profitable has also grown. New markets have opened while others have shrunk. Both through corporate mergers and the undirected demands of international markets, the industry has taken giant steps toward "globalization." As these changes continue to take place, the book publishing industry looks over its collective shoulder at the world of electronic commerce and information exchange and tries to read the future of the book.

Superstores, blockbuster bestsellers, international mergers, the Internet—these are not just the stuff of headlines. They reflect a rapidly changing world, and they necessarily influence the daily decisions of every publisher, whether small or large: how much to invest in a project, which manuscripts to choose, how many to print, and how and where to find buyers for particular works.

With its optimistic title, this book tries to offer a thorough introduction to basic book marketing techniques within our changing world. I believe the principles and concrete suggestions are solid, but in a world that is changing as much as ours, what worked this morning may not work this afternoon. By tomorrow we will have entirely new challenges, and except for our wits, we will probably need an entirely new set of tools to address those problems. Short of foretelling the future, the best strategy is to be as aware as possible of changes taking place, to maintain an experimental stance and to be ready to try new methods and adapt our thinking.

Beyond this enjoinder to flexibility, there is one piece of advice that I want to share with everyone engaged in the joyful and difficult business of publishing. Presumably you are in this business because you have some enthusiasm for something that can be found in books generically and in the particular books you are publishing. In my official role as your marketing guide for the duration of this book, I need to point out that your enthusiasm is not enough. You need readers—and more specifically, bookbuyers—who share that enthusiasm. Your job is to find those people. In today's fiercely competitive and changing marketplace, where everyone is inundated with choices, you must have the ability to reach out and touch an audience.

I am trying to describe the act of book marketing in as palpable and physical terms as I can because it expresses a vitally important fact: The world in which we live is large and impersonal, and your prospective buyers have a multitude of books to choose from as well as other sources of information and media. You need to provide a lot of help—also known as marketing—if you want them to find and select your titles.

INFORMED STRATEGIES

In this book I will show you how to encourage readers to buy your books through effective marketing, and while I hope this book will be useful for everyone involved in book publishing—from entry-level marketing assistants at large houses to their executive bosses—I have tried particularly to address the concerns of small and midsize publishers, authors, and self-publishers. For this reason, I have drawn most of my examples from small publishers who are their own marketing departments or who work with a small staff, as well as those authors who, out of joy or necessity, have taken on a share of the marketing of their own works.

I am addressing the nitty-gritty of book marketing for those who are engaged in the nitty-gritty of attracting buyers for the books with which they work. By way of disclaimer, I would like to say that though the title for this book carries the word "complete," I know, and I'm sure you presume, it won't answer all your questions. I try above all to offer a framework that will help you envision strategies for the marketing of any title, series, or imprint. At the same time I attempt to provide a handle on the methods that will be encompassed in those strategies. Beyond that, I suggest other useful resources for further information.

One further word about the focus of this book: Because the marketing of textbooks is so specialized, and in most respects so divorced from trade and professional publishing, I have chosen not to address this side of the book industry. The strategies that follow primarily focus on trade and professional publishers. Publishers in both camps will find this book useful, especially if they are concerned with expanding their markets. I do, however, briefly discuss the elhi market and the supplementary text market in chapter 8, and I suggest that publishers not overlook these potentially lucrative avenues for sales.

PUBLISHERS AND AUTHORS WORKING TOGETHER

Horror stories, complaints, ill will, frustration, grief: These seem to be the norm in author/publisher relations. Authors, having spent years toiling over a book and expecting to be compensated proportionately (if not monetarily, at least in recognition), are aghast when their book seems to go into the world without any marketing effort on the part of the publisher. When, perhaps six months later, book sales quietly die, their distress turns to horror and feelings of betrayal. On the other hand, publishers feel harassed by authors who have no understanding of their place in the publishing process, who eat up time with unjust complaints, and who interfere when they should be helping.

Both are right. The problem, strangely enough for people whose job is communication, stems from a lack of communication. Authors often don't know what publishers do or how they operate, and so they don't even know what questions to ask. Publishers, on the other hand, struggling with the concerns of business in an ever more competitive environment, forget that the authors with whom they work know little, if anything, about how books are marketed.

This book should help to rectify this unhappy situation.

Addressing publishers, I suggest that they share this book with their authors, offering some words to this effect: "We think you have written a wonderful book and would like to see it succeed, but our marketing resources are limited. Chapters x and y describe the avenues we normally follow, which we consider worthwhile and cost-effective for marketing your book. Nevertheless, for your book to reach its sales potential, your active involvement is necessary. There are marketing strategies described in this book that you can pursue on your own and/or with some help from us. Please read these specific chapters and see what you can do. Then let's talk about what else might be possible."

To authors who have picked up this book on their own, I would like to say the following: You really should have a basic understanding of book publishing and marketing. Read the entire book carefully, but know that, depending on your publisher and your book, only some of the marketing strategies described here will be appropriate and/or cost-effective. Talk to your publisher about his standard procedures. Let him know what you are willing and able to do, and show him that you are in earnest by taking the initiative and doing some of it. Publishers are used to having authors complain that they don't do enough marketing. They are hardened to these complaints, however, because authors often don't do their part. Authors who are skilled and work hard at marketing are a boon to a publisher and will eventually be appreciated and supported, but only after demonstrating the ability to promote their work effectively.

1

Book Marketing Boot Camp

As with every pursuit, book marketing has its own set of conventions and special vocabulary. I was reminded of this recently when I was speaking to a journalist about "co-op" and was met with a look of incomprehension and the question, "Co-op what?" For a moment I was lost; then I realized that the modifier, "marketing and advertising funds," wasn't at all evident. Nor was there any reason why my companion should have been aware that publishers have traditionally offered to share (i.e., cooperate or co-op) in a book-seller's advertising and marketing expenses for promoting particular titles. Nevertheless, having supplied this explanation, my listener was quite at home with the concept.

Book marketing is, after all, neither wholly different from marketing other products or services, nor wholly the same. Certain basic principles apply, albeit with variations. I begin here with a few more or less universal marketing concepts, because many people involved in publishing have no prior marketing experience. Nevertheless, because the central focus of this book is the business of book publishing, I move quickly to the specifics of this strange, wonderful, and rapidly changing industry.

THE DIFFERENCE BETWEEN SALES AND MARKETING

Since for many people the distinction between these two terms is unclear—and because the pursuits of marketing and sales overlap in so many ways—I want to emphasize the practical importance of observing this distinction.

Occasionally, I have been approached by a publisher or self-published author who puts a book in front of me and says, "I need your help in marketing this book." I have responded in most cases by correcting them with the words, "You mean, having bypassed the opportunity for marketing advice, you want me to help you sell this book."

Real marketing begins at the moment you conceive the central idea for the intended book and includes a clear sense of who the book is for, how it serves its audience, and how it fits with the competition. That's why I titled the introduction to this book "Marketing Is Everything." Perhaps I'm guilty of hyperbole, but I think it is important to emphasize that marketing really does touch everything you do—from the book you choose to write and publish, to your choice of packaging, to the title you give it, to the price you charge.

Marketing begins with knowledge of how and where the book will be sold and involves creating a plan and methods for reaching readers—just those elements most people think of as marketing. Nevertheless, because a conventional "marketing plan" is created downstream chronologically from authorial, editorial, and publishing decisions, it is dependent on these decisions. I want to emphasize here that you can't repair a mistake in the book by selling more copies, and you can't repair a marketing mistake in title or price or concept by selling harder.

It may be the idea for your book is so original and timely and the execution so good that the book breaks all bounds, that people see it and love it and tell all their friends about it, and that, despite your lack of planning, you have a success. This has happened. Nevertheless, occasional instances of unplanned success don't argue for not planning. You're more likely to get it right on purpose than by accident.

MAXIMIZING REVENUES

During the almost twenty-five years that I have been involved in book publishing, I have heard certain ideas and phrases repeated. One goes something like this: As a small publisher I can print x thousand copies of a book (the value of x has risen over the years) and still make money, whereas "New York" (the West Coast generic for large corporate publishing) needs to sell three, four, five times that many in order to break even.

There is some truth to this. Some. We will take a brief look at how to determine the numbers you need to meet your financial goals in this chapter. Although I continue to hear this phrase repeated and even see it quoted occasionally in one form or another in *Publishers Weekly*, I have nonetheless observed lots of small publishers shouldering the burdens of low sales, narrow margins, and heavy return rates. My response, whether as a staff marketing director or consultant, has been to seek to maximize the sales of every book.

In the following chapters, I describe a wide range of markets and marketing techniques. While an understanding of each of these is a prerequisite for developing an effective marketing plan, I don't think you will find any voodoo trick or magic formula. Primarily these techniques require knowledge, persistence, and some imagination.

When I'm called upon for marketing help, my first response is to look at the book or books and try to visualize the potential buyers. Who are they? Where can they be found? What do they want? I also spend some time drawing out the author and/or publisher about the book and its audience. There's a joke that a consultant is someone who borrows your watch to tell you the time. In truth, this does describe one aspect of my work. For, whether as a consultant or on staff, the job of the marketing person is to absorb the essence of a book, understand its appeal to a potential audience, and then bring the two together.

Having informed myself as much as possible about a book, my second step is to go through a checklist that includes all of the techniques and markets described in the following chapters to decide which might apply. Most successful publishers today draw revenues from a lot of sources: foreign sales, subsidiary rights, specialty markets, sales direct to consumers, and college course adoptions, as well as the book trade. If at the end of the year your margin is 5 or 10 percent, then the 2 or 3 percent of sales that went to a few of these markets was the difference between profit and loss. Follow every lead you can.

Having been involved in book marketing for many years, I naturally rely on certain techniques and tend to expect results in certain places. Nevertheless, I do also try to think outside the box, and this is where being a good listener helps. I have found over the years that some of my best ideas come from others—especially those with expertise in other subjects and different markets. I would like to emphasize the importance of being open to new possibilities, to listening to authors who know their audience, and to exploring new markets.

MAKING YOUR EFFORTS COST-EFFECTIVE

Most people in business quickly realize that it's easier to increase sales than profitability. If you spend more money on marketing, your sales should increase. The trick, especially when you're marketing books, is to make your marketing cost-effective, and that can be a real feat. You're dealing with a relatively low-priced item, high discounts, returns (something that most other businesses don't have to deal with), and, worst of all, the lack of repeat buyers. Rarely do you sell more than one copy of a book to a consumer, and it's even difficult to sell several different books to one buyer.

Having spent my career working with small- and medium-sized publishers for whom every dollar counts, I am acutely sensitive to the need for appropriate-scale marketing efforts. If the concept of strategy means anything in book marketing, it means this: to select and find methods that result in a profitable book and a profitable company.

Obviously this is a goal that cannot be reached by marketing alone. If you waste money on production or your overhead is excessively high, you can't expect clever marketing to make up the difference. If you're a publisher, your marketing efforts are one piece in a complex system called a business. If you're an author, the whole process becomes simpler. Unless your book is a promotional tool for other services you offer, you simply can't spend more per sale than will be returned in royalties.

So how do you decide how much to spend, and on what? I don't have one simple answer, but as you go through this book you should find that some of the strategies and some of the markets will seem appropriate for your book or your company, while others won't apply. You need to make some projections and calculations and some guesses. Experience helps a lot. If you've tried something and gotten certain results, you can do some interpolation and extrapolation and make more accurate projections than you could for an entirely new strategy.

One word of advice: Keep some records on what you've tried and what the results were. I never cease to be amazed at how haphazard seemingly sophisticated publishers can be when it comes to their marketing expenditures. Instinct and common sense are, of course, invaluable assets, especially where marketing is concerned, but information ranks next to these, and it can be the critical element in making your marketing cost-effective.

CALCULATING THE FINANCIAL PARAMETERS

Though most book publishers enter the publishing business out of a love for books, the business side of publishing soon occupies a major portion of their time and energy. This is natural, if not entirely congenial. Except for those with unlimited resources, the numbers, to a large extent, will govern what they can publish, how much they can publish, and how well they will be able to market their books.

To maintain a viable business and monitor the financial health of a company, publishers need to create and maintain a series of financial tools—cash flow projections, detailed income statements (tracking income and expenditures by category and department), and balance sheets. These not only help you stay in business, but also give advance warning if some aspect of your basic publishing plan isn't working.

While the proper financial management of a publishing company is beyond the scope of this book, in the following pages I present one simple financial tool, a profitability analysis that should be used for each book. Skipping this process not only courts disaster but also guarantees that you won't learn from either your mistakes or your successes. I discuss this tool, rather than those mentioned above, because it is intimately involved in your expectations for your books and for the marketing money you will assign to each title.

I have heard publishers say that because the numbers in such an analysis can be manipulated to say anything, they don't want to engage in making these projections. I respond by saying that though it is true you can make a questionable book look profitable on paper before it is published, you will have the piece of paper to consult for the next book and the next and the next. Whoever justified the last disaster by projecting sales for a book that lost money will be forced to recognize their accountability when called upon the next time. Naturally, projecting sales accurately will always be difficult, and you'll always miss on some titles. Nevertheless, it is better to err on the conservative side. Lots of books that could have made a profit result in losses because publishers paid the author too high an advance and printed too many copies. Finally, you had better know just how many you need to sell to meet your financial goals, and you should get as much feedback as you can about whether you can realistically make the number you project.

A Model Profitability Analysis

While the numbers in the following analysis will vary for each book and every publisher, the method and format should work in most cases. I have seen various versions of these forms, some more readable than others and some more detailed. If your operation contains elements not included here, find a way to include them.

What if, for instance, as a publisher of professional books, you sell direct to consumers and actually make a profit on the shipping charges? In this case, you need to add a line under the heading "other sources of income." It doesn't really matter what kind of format you use, as long as all the relevant factors have been accounted for and you can refer to them when examining the impact of price and print-run changes.

Also keep in mind that almost every line on the following form will be affected by the nature of your individual operation and requires some thought. The nature of your business and your trade practices will have a direct and substantial effect on factors that at first glance seem to be standard. The following are some representative guidelines and issues to consider when developing and working with your profitability analysis:

- **Trade sales and returns** Are you losing money on returned books, or will they be sent out again and finally sold? What percentage of returns is unsalable? Are you actually collecting for damaged copies, or will you take the loss on damages? Will you remainder unsold and damaged books? If so, you should have an income line for the amount you will receive from remainder sales. If you print conservatively, charge accounts for damaged books, and continue to sell a book until it is out of print, then even if you have normal trade returns, your returns line might be very small. Even so, you can have significant costs in processing the returns, and you will need a method for assigning these.

- **Projected period of sales** Note that the sample form reproduced here, while useful for projecting your return on investment, contains no provision for the length of time it will take you to sell out the first printing. If you always attempt to print for a particular length of time and are pretty good at projecting, you can rely on a formula. If you expect large variations, you must create a method for figuring in this possibility.

- **Distributor statements** If you're working with a full-service distributor, the distributor's fees will include both sales commissions and salaries as well as all the costs of warehousing and fulfillment. You can make some estimates of how to assign these costs, or for simplicity, you can include them as lump sum representing the cost of trade sales.

- **Marketing and editorial overhead** In addition to contracted costs, each book you publish takes staff time. You should have a way to track these costs and include them. In the example that follows, I have simply tucked departmental staff time into the "other" categories.

- **Assigning costs to frontlist and backlist** Because this kind of financial analysis is usually run only on frontlist titles, you should make some adjustment in figuring how much of your overhead and administrative costs are borne by the backlist; otherwise you will make new publishing projects look more expensive than they are.

- **Cost of money** While your cost of borrowing is presumably included in the general and administrative costs, if you are considering a book that is extremely expensive and will sell more slowly than most of the books in your line, you will need to figure in the cost of money as a separate item rather than rely on the same formula you usually use.

Title: *Everybody's Guide to Left Bank Mergers and Acquisitions*
Cover price: $18.95
Specs:
Trade paper, 6″ × 9″, 256 pages, no illustrations,
   ISBN: 0-12345-678-9
Pub. date: May 2000
First printing: 10,000 copies

	Copies	Dollars
Sales:		
Trade sales (at 49% average discount)	7,000	$68,000
− Returns	700	$ 7,000
= Net trade sales	6,300	$61,000
Direct sales (at full price)	1,000	$20,000
Other sales (at 35% average discount)	1,000	$12,000
= Total sales	8,300	$93,000
Other sources of income:		
Book club royalties (at 50% pub. share)	800	$ 2,000
Foreign rights		$ 3,000
Other subsidiary rights		0
= Total other income		$ 5,000
= Total income		$98,000

Cost of goods:	
Paper, printing, and binding (Pp&b) and freight	$20,000
Royalties (including advance)	$16,000
= Total cost of goods	$36,000
Operating expenses:	
Development costs:	
Editorial	$ 4,000
Production	$ 3,000
Other development costs	$ 2,000
Marketing and sales costs:	
Public relations	$ 5,000
Direct mail	$ 4,000
Free copies	$ 1,000
Commissions	$ 4,000
Other marketing costs	$ 7,000
Fulfillment costs	$11,000
General and administrative costs	$ 8,000
= Total operating costs	$49,000
Total income	$98,000
– Total expenses	$85,000
= Net income (or loss)	$13,000

How Much Should You Spend?

What's the typical marketing and sales budget for a trade or professional publisher? I've seen and heard of numbers ranging anywhere from 10 percent of net sales to 25 percent, and I've also seen 18 percent quoted as an average. These figures included sales commissions of trade books as well as all other marketing expenditures. How much you spend will depend on many factors, including the kind of publishing you're doing, your cash flow, your plans for expansion, and the percent of your income that comes from backlist and frontlist.

I know one publisher who has consistently invested in marketing at the high end of this range, sacrificing profits in the short term to help build the reputation of the company. The result has been consistently larger sales for titles than one might expect, and the success of these books has in turn helped attract more established authors to the list. At some point, it will probably be necessary to increase the company's margin, but as a growth strategy investing in more marketing has proven successful.

PUT YOUR MARKETING PLAN ON PAPER

Unless you are a start-up publisher, your marketing plans for forthcoming titles will naturally be rooted in your ongoing activities. If you publish professional reference volumes and you have an active direct-mail program, you know your new titles will find a place in your direct-mail catalog. If you regularly attend professional association meetings, you know which of your new books will be displayed at which meetings. And if you rely heavily on publicity to create pull through bookstores, you know your new trade titles will be supported by public-relations campaigns.

In each instance, however, the question remains: How much will you spend on a particular title, and if you target multiple channels, how will you proportion your expenses? Depending on the size and complexity of your company, answering these questions can involve either a few simple projections or juggling a long list of conflicting demands for the allocation of scarce funds. Whatever your situation, I counsel the same overriding principles that I recommended in the preparation of your title profitability analysis: be conservative, thorough, and systematic. Create a budget and marketing plan and put them on paper.

You begin this plan with two basic pieces of information: your target audience and your sales expectations. Proceed by looking at the different methods you have for reaching your audience and what these methods will cost. If you rely almost exclusively on direct mail, for instance, you can look at the cost and availability of appropriate lists, decide if you want to promote a title by itself, and project the size and cost of initial mailings. You can also budget for follow-up mailings that kick in at a certain response rate. If, on the other hand, you promote a group of books in each direct-mail package, you must assign a percentage of the mailing cost to each book based on the percentage of space allotted to that title in the catalog, brochure, letter, or other element of the mailing package. The books you expect to do best will naturally be featured more prominently and more often; however, with a budget and a marketing plan, how much more won't be a matter of chance, but of planning.

Similarly, if you sell almost entirely through the trade and rely on publicity to attract buyers, you will need to budget a percentage of your publicist's time or the services of a freelance publicist, the cost of review copies, travel expenses for a tour, and so forth. Books and authors at the top of the list will once again be awarded a larger budget and more opportunities.

All of this is relatively straightforward. While every sales projection is subject to error, you can do these computations without using calculus. Even publishers that target several major markets and utilize a range of marketing vehicles must ask and answer questions that involve the relative costs of different programs and their expectations of success.

The key here—and the reason it is so important to create a formal marketing plan—is to take the time to consider your options and commitment when you make the decision to publish a book. I stated above that in developing your marketing plan it is important to be conservative. Nevertheless, it is also crucial to be enthusiastic, optimistic, and creative. You, as publisher, marketer, or author, have to sit down and visualize the ways you can reach readers. This is the moment to think outside the box. All the clichés about aiming high apply here. It's unlikely that you'll exceed your goals, and in the day-to-day press of getting things done you're less likely to be inventive. Moreover, even if you think of a clever way to market the book later, you've already committed your marketing funds.

Returning to the hypothetical book for which we did a model profitability analysis, our marketing plan might look something like this:

Sample Marketing Plan for *Everybody's Guide to Left Bank Mergers and Acquisitions*

Description and audience:

This is an anecdotal book about interesting deals, not a technical how-to. We feel this book will appeal to general business readers— executives and entrepreneurs—attracted to anecdotal stories of finance and arbitrage and who want to understand the context in which such deals are created. We think the book will do well in the trade, is a natural for the popular business press, and will do moderately well through our business direct-mail program. The work and the market seem comparable to several previous books we have published, *Bank is a Four-Letter Word* (fourteen thousand copies sold in trade paper over three years) and last season's *My Life in Investment Banking* (seventy-five hundred sold in cloth in six months, but we haven't seen the returns). We sold about one thousand copies of the former through direct mail and twenty-five hundred of the latter to our core list of bank executives.

Because of the popular nature of this book, we see the banking community as a secondary rather than primary market. The author is confident of receiving testimonial quotes from a few well-known arbitrageurs as well as a former French cabinet minister. If these quotes materialize, we will probably do better with the secondary markets.

Author:

With solid academic and consulting credentials, our author has a modest but good reputation among his professional colleagues. While this is his first book for a popular audience, he has authored several professional texts and articles for some of the leading popular business magazines.

Public relations:

While we will focus primarily on print reviews, we will give the author a limited tour to New York, Washington, D.C., Philadelphia, and Boston. Since the author lives and teaches in the New York area, these are all relatively short hops, and the author has agreed to pay his own travel expenses. In addition, the author will be addressing professional meetings in Houston in August and Duluth in December, so we will try to set up some additional media while he is in those cities. Budget: $5,000.

Book clubs:

We will be submitting to all the business-oriented clubs. Our sub-rights manager has spoken with Jane Doe at the Bigger and Better Book Club who has expressed interest.

Professional meetings and trade shows:

This book will be on our A-list at BEA, and we will have a display of the cover. We will also be displaying at the professional meetings we regularly attend. At the Duluth meeting we will offer a special professional discount and have the author sign books in our booth. Budget: $750.

Direct mail:

This will be our lead title in the Fall Business-Book Mailing that goes to our house list. We will also promote the book in three other mailings during fall and winter. Budget: $4,000.

Bookstore promotions:

We have targeted this book for an "Adventures in High Finance" endcap promotion for the chain that will feature all our books, including this one. We are also offering co-op. Budget: $4,000.

Advertising:

Along with other A-list titles, this book will be featured in our annual full-page ad in the BEA issue of *Publishers Weekly*. We don't plan any other advertising. As is our policy, if we get a very good review in either *Library Journal* or *Booklist*, we will support library sales with a small ad in the appropriate periodical. Budget: $250.

Start Marketing Now

While emphasizing that the largest conception of marketing includes everything you will do as a publisher, I know how overwhelming it is to try to get everything done. Once you've decided to publish the book and put it in your schedule, the clock starts ticking—not just for the author, who is trying to get the manuscript in on time, but for the marketing staff, who can begin their work on the book a full year before the scheduled publication. In concluding this first chapter, therefore, I provide a sample checklist that includes many of the conventional marketing activities pursued by trade publishers. Use it as the basis for creating your own.

MARKETING TIMELINE

Six to twelve months before publication:
- Offer sale of first serial rights to periodicals—send selected chapters, excerpts, or manuscript with table of contents and cover letter

Seven months before publication:
- Begin cover design

Six months before publication:
- Submit Advance Book Information (ABI) to R. R. Bowker for inclusion in *Books in Print* (forms available from the Bowker Web site at *www.bowker.com*)

Four to six months before publication:
- Produce cover art (printed covers or color photos of mock-up for sales conference)
- Write editorial fact sheet, back cover, and trade catalog copy
- Submit to book clubs

Four months before publication:
- Write press release/create press kit (photo, author bio, backgrounder, sample questions, clippings; all as appropriate)
- Send galleys with press release to prepublication reviewers: *Publishers Weekly*, *Library Journal*, *Booklist*, *Kirkus*, and newspapers with pullout review sections. (You should have "guidelines" for submissions from the above magazines for reference. Also make sure you have current, correct name of editor.)
- Begin work on prepub direct-mail offer

Three months before publication:
- Send galleys with cover letter and press release to specialty catalogs and any special sales outlets

- Send galleys with cover letter and press release to periodicals for review or second serial rights
- Make follow-up phone calls on any or all of the above as soon as three weeks after mailing

Two months before publication:

- Mail prepub direct-mail offers
- Pull media lists and prepare press kits for PR campaign

One month before publication:

- Ensure that books are in stock

Three weeks before publication:

- Send out press kits for author interviews, send review copies with press release and cover letter, and follow up with phone calls ten to fourteen days after shipping (if sent UPS or first class)

After publication:

- Your marketing activities can continue after publication as long as they remain cost-effective

2

Fundamental Strategies
for Your Book, List,
and Company

I began this book by saying that "marketing is everything" in order to emphasize that some of your most important marketing decisions concern what are often considered editorial choices. Is this book effective? Is it written well? Is there an audience? If your answer is no to any of these questions, presumably you wouldn't publish the book.

Having answered these questions in the affirmative, you now need to develop strategies that give your company and each book you publish the best possible chance for success.

CREATE A PACKAGE THAT ATTRACTS BUYERS

Despite technological advances offering publishers the opportunity to enhance the value of a book through attractive physical packaging, most books are still primarily plain pages of type wrapped between colorful covers. Nevertheless, whether your work tends toward a highly visual format or you are primarily working with straight text-based works, questions of packaging design can influence your profitability. Even if you are committed to the simplest 6″ × 9″ format and unadorned pages of type, you should at least be aware of your options and how they might play out in the marketplace. Some years ago I heard the late Ian Ballantine, noted as the father of the paperback revolution, remark that the future of the book was in the use of visuals.

Whether this prediction still stands is hard to say. Nevertheless, packaging choices, which have become increasingly complex over the last ten or twenty years, have become increasingly important as physical books meet ever greater competition from electronic media. Oversize books, tiny books, oblong books, perforated collections of postcards, pop-up books, lavishly illustrated coffee-table books, two-color texts, unusual interior design—all of these have a market and a place in contemporary publishing.

Imaginative Editorial Equals Effective Marketing

How often do editors sign up seemingly good books that proceed straight to the remainder table because an imagined audience wasn't really there? Conversely, the editor who understands the audience for a book and creates a package that maximizes its appeal to that audience adds value to the author's words.

At the University of Georgia Press, the opportunity to develop a new concept, the "environmental gift book," not only proved successful in broadening a core target audience of environmentalist readers but opened new marketing doors for a relatively small academic publisher.

The idea for these books began through a collaboration between noted nature writer Barry Lopez and illustrator Tom Pohrt on a book titled *Lessons from the Wolverine*. The pair brought the idea to Barbara Ras, senior editor at the press, who had worked with both before, and presented a project they conceived of as a "small illustrated gift book." For Ras—whose acquisitions area included the environment, nature, and regional trade titles—the idea was a perfect fit. She brought in noted book designer David

---

Bullen, and set in motion a collaborative process with each member of the team shaping the final book.

Launched at the BEA, *Lessons from the Wolverine* brought immediate benefits to the publisher. Lopez was featured on a BEA panel discussing writer and artist collaborations—a slot a small publisher would not normally have access to—and also signed books at the publisher's booth.

A second, more long-range benefit was to attract another prominent writer, Rick Bass, who approached the press about doing a book in a similar format. The result was *Fiber*, a passionate preservationist work with illustrations by Elizabeth Hughes Bass. Here, once again, the combination of powerful language and evocative illustrations created a graceful, beautiful book that reached out to a broader audience than would have responded to the text alone. Filling out what had now become a "mini-series" was another book by Lopez, *Apologia*, this time with woodcut illustrations by Robin Eschner, and a work by Frank Soos, *Bamboo Fly Rod Suite: Reflections on Fishing and the Geography of Grace*, with illustrations by Kesler Woodward.

While none of these titles was ever in danger of breaking onto a bestseller list, they have brought the University of Georgia Press increased media attention and raised bookseller awareness of the publisher's offerings. Because of these titles, the press opened new accounts with bookstores that previously had simply overlooked the publisher. These stores have in turn ordered a range of books where they did no business before.

THE TITLE IS THE BOOK YOU BUY

You may or may not be able to tell a book by its cover, but one thing is for sure, people choose books by their titles, especially nonfiction books. Where fiction is concerned, it may be the case that a poetic title will be easier to remember, and a poetic or suggestive title that evokes the mood of the work or a central memorable image may connect with a potential reader, but it's less critical in the buying decision than genre, or author reputation, or setting, or even the style of the work itself. Since people buy fiction because they have heard of the author or are familiar with the book through a recommendation or review, whether a novel is called *Cold Mountain* or *The Color Purple* or *The God of Small Things* probably isn't a major factor in a buying decision.

With nonfiction, however, people commonly look for more information from a title than with fiction. While poetic titles are, of course, still common for nonfiction—*Into Thin Air, The Color of Water,* and *A Distant Mirror*—precise descriptive titles abound, such as *Seven Habits of Highly Effective People, The New York Public Library Desk Reference,* and *Lindbergh.* Nevertheless, even where a publisher chooses to go with a poetic title, the title is usually clarified by a descriptive subtitle. The subtitle for *Into Thin Air* reads: *A Personal Account of the Mount Everest Disaster,* for *The Color of Water* it's: *A Black Man's Tribute to His White Mother,* and for *A Distant Mirror,* it's: *The Calamitous Fourteenth Century.* Clearly, publishers are concerned that potential readers know exactly what a book is about.

This method of titling and subtitling is effective for the bookstore, where a book will be shelved by category and the browser can quickly make out the title, subtitle, and even several levels of sell copy. It becomes less effective, however, when the book appears in catalogs, Internet listings, or is the subject of passing references. As these sales methods become more important, publishers tend to rely on a clear descriptive title to attract the attention of potential buyers. Authors and publishers need to think about how their titles will be used, not just what sounds good.

All this said, a really good title can and does add value to the publishing process, attracting readers with a concept or phrase that speaks to their interests, needs, or desires. Among my personal favorites are:

Fifty Simple Things You Can Do to Save the Earth
Getting Things Done When You Are Not in Charge
Men Are from Mars, Women Are from Venus

The first is, perhaps, my all-time favorite. Simple, clear, direct, and effectively using the second person, the title proffers both a challenge and a solution on a subject of universal concern. The second—

while less successful in my mind because it has mistakenly avoided "how to" in favor of the gerund—still works because it offers a solution to a seemingly universal problem. Both of these titles took my breath away the first time I heard them. Although it is very different from the first two, I was nevertheless instantly taken by the title *Men Are from Mars, Women Are from Venus*. Dense with associations, vivid, and interesting, my only concern was whether the book could match the wit of the title.

THE COVER SELLS THE BOOK

While most people are happy to repeat the adage that you can't tell a book by its cover, there is certainly no doubt in the minds of most publishers that people do in fact buy books because of their covers. Knowing that fact, however, still leaves open the question of what is an effective cover? Having participated in innumerable cover discussions where directly opposing points of view were expressed, I'm well aware of the subjectivity that goes into a cover choice. I also know that styles and tastes change regularly, so that what works for one season may soon be outmoded.

Being neither inclined nor equipped to lay out aesthetic principles for cover designs, I would like to offer a few basic practical concerns that publishers should keep in mind when working with designers.

Make it Legible

Having spent a fair amount of time writing copy for dust jackets, direct-mail projects, and other kinds of packaging, I've engaged in the seemingly inevitable tug-of-war that takes place between writers and designers. Writers want more copy. Designers want more space, more visual drama, and more, in a word, "design." As the publisher or marketer, it's often your job to mediate this competition. Beyond the conflict of words versus space, however, there is a more important consideration: legibility. If the title and subtitle of a book are hard to read, whether on the front or spine, the cover has failed in its basic purpose. Effective design aids the reader. When considering a cover, I always take a few steps back to see what it looks like from five or ten feet away. If I can still read the title and subtitle, it passes the legibility test.

*Make Sure the Cover Is Clear
When Reproduced in Black-and-White*

If at any time black-and-white photos of your books are featured in reviews, flyers, catalogs, or space ads, you want the cover image to be clear and the title legible. This is an obvious point, but it is often forgotten during consideration of cover designs. If you're looking at color comps of prospective covers, take them over to your black-and-white copy machine and see how they reproduce. Your machine copy will probably lose a lot more detail than a printed photo, and it will probably smudge contrasting hues more, too, but looking at a black-and-white machine copy will give you a way to imagine what a photo of your book will look like on newsprint. Is your beautiful, subtle, evocative cover still interesting? And is it still legible, or did the bright yellow title disappear into the surrounding field?

Make Sure the Title Is Legible at Thumbnail Size

All the same criteria apply in this test as above. Photos of covers are often reproduced in quite small sizes for all kinds of uses. I've seen lots of catalogs and ads where the book titles only appear as they are in cover photos and are omitted from the catalog copy. If the title isn't legible in the cover photo, readers can't determine the name of the book described in the accompanying copy. In such cases, the catalog listing or ad has been completely wasted.

*Make Sure Your Cover Is Clear
at Thumbnail Size on a Computer Screen*

This one is a recent addition to my list, but given the growth in Internet bookselling, an important consideration. Fortunately, you can rely on reasonable color and contrast for the most part, so this test is easier to pass than the black-and-white test and probably coincides with the thumbnail test. Nevertheless, you should test your design to be sure.

Effective Cover Copy

For many shoppers, bookstore browsing consists of a narrowing process. They are drawn to the featured displays at the front of the store, or perhaps they want a book on a particular topic and browse only that area. Or, being in the store with the general desire to find something entertaining, they meander among the sections that consistently attract them. They pick a book off the shelf because the title sounds interesting or they know who the author is. They glance briefly at the cover—registering a fleeting positive or negative impression—and they turn the book over to read the back cover.

For publisher and author, this is an important moment. Some will decide this is not the book they want and put it back on the shelf without ever having read a word of the actual contents. Others, who find the back cover inviting or interesting, will proceed to open the book and sample the contents. Good cover copy will draw your potential reader in.

So, what works for cover copy? This will naturally vary with the kind of title at hand. Most fiction titles rely on a simple description of the setting and plot. Certain kinds of nonfiction call for third-person descriptive copy, others work best with copy in the second person and present tense. In general, observe the basic principles of good sales copy. Use simple, clear, direct language, and emphasize what's strong, new, or different.

Though seemingly overdone, testimonial quotes and/or reviews provide credibility and reassurance to your potential buyers. Use them wherever a strong quote is available from a recognizable source. I usually don't recommend including anonymous quotes, such as "from D.C. in California," nor do I recommend a back cover that uses only quotes. Your strongest cover will combine credible recommendations with some descriptive copy that summarizes as strongly as possible the legitimate value of the book.

A Book Is a Thing

In article after article about e-commerce and the seemingly inevitable evolution toward the electronic delivery of information, there is always a quote from a publishing professional who remarks how much he loves the feel of books and how he will miss the smell of ink on paper and the wonderful "fetishistic" properties of a printed book. Given the universality of this sentiment, printed books are probably not destined to disappear in the near term.

Whatever the future holds, publishers must in the meantime do whatever they can to provide satisfying and appropriate packaging for the works they publish while balancing the cost of enhanced production values. Bulkier paper, though a little more expensive, can support a higher price for a thin volume. A more attractive cover and interior design may or may not cost more, but again adds value. Nonstandard trim sizes and illustrations and photos all add distinction and can justify their cost. Design and marketing do not simply overlap. Design is an important piece in your overall marketing strategy.

KNOW THE COMPETITION

In response to a question after her talk, I once heard a buyer for one of the major chains comment that she never ceased to be amazed at the number of books being published annually or at the number of titles competing for shelf space. She went on to say, however, that she had felt that way even more strongly when she first entered the business many years before. She concluded that since such a vast number of books had been successfully published in the intervening years, and so many new publishers had thrived, the mere presence of competition shouldn't necessarily discourage a publisher or an author.

While the point is well made, I would like to add a question: Over the years, how many books and publishers have failed because they couldn't compete? Though I don't have an answer regarding the quantity, I know that those who failed to live up to expectations did so for several reasons. Some failed because they simply weren't good enough. Others failed because they were competing against titles that were better marketed. Finally, there were some that came along too late in a cycle of interest or at the end of a fad.

If a book enters the marketplace and there are already a number of recently well-established titles, the new book needs the muscle to push the others aside—a better-known author, a new angle, better packaging, or a lot of marketing exposure. If the newest addition is obviously inferior to several books already on the market, even a lower price point is unlikely to help. If, on the other hand, your book includes information previously unavailable, establishes a new approach, or is authored by someone who has recently attained a position of prominence in a profession, there's a good reason why a buyer would want your book rather than, or even in addition to, others already on the shelf.

Similarly, if you're dealing with a subject that has suddenly exploded in popularity, timing is important. Over the past twenty years the publishing business has seen cycles of rapid expansion and contraction in computer manuals, cookbooks, and illustrated juveniles, to name a few. Obviously all of these categories are strong and will presumably stick around for a long time to come. Nevertheless, each has seen a surge in publishing interest that resulted in overpublishing and a consequent contraction that cost many publishers dearly. If you have the fifteenth or the fiftieth book on the healing power of crystals, it may not matter that it's the best. It's just too late.

As author or publisher you need to know where you fit in the marketplace, gauge your timeliness, and have a strategy for standing out.

PUBLISH FOR THE FRONTLIST AND THE BACKLIST

While a publishing company grows by adding new titles and selling them successfully, for most publishers day-to-day survival depends on the backlist. Margins are better on backlist titles since development costs have already been amortized—returns are lower, and most of the marketing has already been done. With experience, publishers can also predict the rate of sales for a particular title, so they can print efficiently.

A few years ago *Publishers Weekly* ran an article on backlist sales in which they surveyed executives from some of the largest publishers and imprints. These folks gave estimates of backlist sales as a percentage of total sales that ranged from 25 percent (Hyperion) at the low end to 75 percent (Modern Library) and 80 percent (Sterling) at the high end.

Though there is no one-size-fits-all solution to this problem, my own experience in observing a great many publishers suggests that it's extremely difficult to break even in this business—let alone make a profit—with less than 50 percent of sales derived from the backlist. Certainly the size of your company and the nature of your line will affect your breakeven point. Nevertheless, as a rule of thumb I suggest that publishers set this figure as a minimum goal and allocate their resources accordingly.

The challenge, of course, is to publish titles that will continue to sell over the long term, and here reference publishers, professional publishers, and niche publishers have the advantage. Dealing with specialty information and a specialized audience, they have a good sense of the total current market, what percentage they can sell initially, and how many new customers enter the market each year. A travel guide, for instance, though it competes in a tough market and may require regular updating, can sell year after year as new visitors choose the destination. Similarly, a guide for new owners of an exotic pet may sell the same in its fifth year as in its first.

Those who are selling less price-sensitive books can also adopt a hardcover/paperback strategy that maximizes revenues on the initial hardcover printing. By monitoring the sales closely at the outset, publishers can then decide whether to reprint in hardcover, move to paperback, or simply let the book go out of print. Reprinting in paperback also offers the opportunity for some renewed marketing efforts.

DEVOTE SOME OF YOUR PR BUDGET TO BACKLIST TITLES

Contrary to what many believe, a book does not need to be new to attract a radio or television author interview. Most hosts and producers don't care when a book was published. Their only concern is whether the author has something to say that is timely and interesting to their audience. If you have a staff publicist, you can assign a certain percentage of that person's time to setting up radio phoner interviews for backlist authors.

In addition, if you have cultivated a publishing niche, you should also have a database of editors and producers who cover your field. Make the most of your media contacts by promoting your backlist when you mail to them. Years ago, as the public relations director for a publisher of consumer self-help books, I assembled an "A-list" of consumer action reporters. Whenever I sent them a press kit for a new title, I would include a complete catalog. Reporters read through these catalogs and would often pick out books that fit into stories they were already working on. Occasionally they would even decide to do a topical round-up and mention several titles. The overall effect of including these catalogs was incredible.

Key Into Author Efforts

Many authors combine speaking with writing and are on the road a lot. Keep in touch with your authors, get their schedules and arrange media events in the cities they are visiting. Over the course of a year or two, the promotional results can equal your initial marketing push.

When authors have a new book you can take the opportunity to promote their previous titles as well. Readers of fiction will often buy several books by the same author, but nonfiction writers also build up followings. It doesn't matter which book was written first, if I read a book by someone and like it, the chances are good that I will look for others by the same author. Encourage bookstores to stock an author's previous works along with his new books (even if the new book is from another publisher), and include information about previous works, if you've published them, in your press kits. While you don't want to dilute frontlist promotions, you can coach authors to mention their previous works in interviews.

Refresh the Content and the Packaging

Like buildings, books age, although some age more quickly than others. Also like buildings, you can remodel them or give them a facelift—a new cover, a new edition with updated material, and even a new title. Take for example, Huston Smith's classic work, *The Religions of Man*. The book, first published in 1958, became an instant hit and continued to sell well for decades. By 1992, however, the title was no longer acceptable and was changed to *The World's Religions*. With the new title the book remains one of the bestselling works in the genre.

Less radical, but more common than changing a title, publishers can redesign covers on books that continue selling long enough for graphic styles to change. When, for instance, Penguin Classics were first introduced in the forties and fifties, a two-color cover with a simple border and type was adequate. By the late sixties, however, this series was competing with a number of attractively packaged lines and Penguin moved to dramatically illustrated four-color covers.

Publishers with nonfiction titles that feature timely material can extend the life of such books by updating the contents and creating new editions. While subsequent editions won't draw the review attention of a new book, they can be occasions for author interviews and bookstore promotions. By changing at least 25 percent of the content, publishers will also draw orders from librarians who are concerned about providing patrons with current information.

ADVERTISE ONLY WHEN APPROPRIATE

While in some industries advertising and marketing are synonymous, most small and midsize publishers make very limited use of this expensive tool. Reflecting this fact, I relegate my discussion of advertising to this small subsection and limit my discussion to some of the main publisher uses of advertising.

For small publishers, I begin by issuing my standard warning: Large-scale or even small-scale consumer advertising such as that conducted by the major corporate publishers for their lead titles is neither appropriate nor cost-effective for others. Larger publishers that engage in these promotions make a statement to authors, agents, and the industry—a statement that perhaps contributes to their overall success. Smaller publishers tend to use advertising in very special ways. Advertising a high-priced professional or reference book in a trade journal—especially where a toll-free phone number or a direct-response coupon is used—can be cost-effective, as can any campaign where the advertising medium and the book in question are tightly targeted.

Your advertising, if you do budget something for this marketing tool, must produce income, either through increased attention from the trade or from consumers. Here are a few strategies worth considering.

ADVERTISING TO THE TRADE

When advertising in *Publishers Weekly*, *Library Journal*, *Booklist*, and other trade magazines and catalogs, most publishers have a clear purpose: to encourage orders from libraries and bookstores. An important secondary value, especially for the "Announcement" issues of *Publishers Weekly*, is increased attention from agents, purchasers of subrights, and reviewers, all of whom scan the announcement ads for materials relevant to them.

ADVERTISING TO SUPPORT ATTENTION FROM REVIEWERS

The definition of editorial integrity for any publication begins with a firewall between the advertising and editorial departments. You can't buy a review, nor would the review be worth much if you could. Nevertheless, editors do look at the ads in their own magazines, and if you're a regular advertiser they will naturally pay attention to your books when they are submitted for review.

If you're a literary publisher who regularly submits books for review to literary journals, your ads in those journals, whatever impact they make on the journal's readers, do help establish you as a worthy partner for the magazine's staff. Your books will still need to be worthwhile in the editors' minds in order to receive a review, but they will naturally give them full consideration, where otherwise your books might have been lumped with the hundreds of other submissions gathering dust on the office floor.

ADVERTISING TO BUILD PUBLISHER IDENTITY

A strategic tool that is particularly useful to create name recognition for larger publishers, but also relevant for all niche publishers, is advertising in the media for a targeted audience. This can help establish your entire line of books in the minds of reviewers and consumers. Such advertising needs to be consistent, repeated, and frequent. So, if you don't have the budget to meet these criteria, it's probably not worth it to spend on occasional ads.

Five Tips for Cost-Effective Consumer Advertising

While often thought of as the primary purpose of advertising, using ads to encourage consumer purchases normally appears pretty low on a publisher's list of favored marketing and sales techniques. For the most part, the cost-to-sales ratio is just too high. When asked what influences their book-buying decisions, consumers cite advertising extremely infrequently, and most books carry too low a price to justify a costly campaign where there is a low percentage response rate.

If, however, you have books that sell in numbers large enough to justify advertising support, here are some basic guidelines for using your money wisely.

1. **Don't advertise in a vacuum**

    Advertising works best when pursued in conjunction with other kinds of marketing. You can use advertising to boost attendance and responsiveness on author tours, to revive word of mouth after the tour is completed and in the wake of positive reviews.

    Some publishers will plan an advertising campaign around anticipated reviews. They make their plans contingent on getting enough good reviews and cancel if those reviews aren't forthcoming. They understand that the ads are going to be most effective when they support and are supported by positive review activity.

2. **Know why you are advertising**

    Most book advertising serves either to announce the publication of a book that people already want to read or to inform people that a particular book exists. In the case of the latest novel by John Grisham or Danielle Steel, for instance, advertising simply serves to alert an author's fans that a new book is now available.

    These, however, are the exceptions. In most cases you want to attract potential readers to a new title. You want to find the readers who have a demonstrated connection to a particular subject area and inform them about a book they would naturally find interesting. The furthest extension of this strategy, occasionally practiced, might be used to connect with an audience that doesn't usually read or buy books yet would be a logical choice for a particular title because of the content—a book on skateboarding, for instance, could be advertised in *Thrasher*, a magazine targeted to the predominantly young devotees of this sport.

3. **Know your audience**

    As in any marketing effort, understanding your target is essential. Effective advertising demands that you know what will appeal to the most likely buyers of the book you are promoting. You have to establish a strong, compelling message and get that message across in the language and style that is most likely to speak to the hearts and minds of those you want to reach. Hopefully, you defined this audience before you ever made the decision to publish. If so, you know what they read, how the book at hand addresses their tastes or needs, and how to communicate this fact.

4. **Know when to advertise**

   With the growth of just-in-time inventory practices, new titles have an incredibly short window of opportunity in which to establish themselves, so getting your timing right is a tricky business. Your advertising may be more effective after reviews have appeared or at the tail end of the author tour, but if you delay too long you may miss the window.

   For seasonal books, you can create holiday tie-ins—romance publishers, for instance, make a big push around Valentine's Day—with good results. Since a very high percentage of book sales are made during the Christmas season this is the logical time to promote gift books with ads. If you're working on a scale that allows, it can also be wise to allocate some discretionary funds for advertising so you can take advantage of those occasions when a title takes off and can benefit from a quick infusion.

5. **Know where to advertise**

   Newspapers, magazines, radio, television, the Internet, even billboards—the possibilities are vast. Naturally, your choices will be limited to a great extent by your budget, but more important, you need to think through a strategy that maximizes exposure to your target audience. If you have business book, for example, you're more likely to reach potential readers on the business pages of the newspaper or in business magazines rather than on the book review pages. There are magazines and Internet sites that address every conceivable subject, so it's easy to find your niche audiences. If you're looking for quick turnaround or a regional audience, then newspapers are a natural choice. In addition, radio and television, though often underused by publishers, now have a wide range of programming serving niche audiences. With the right book or author, these mediums can be very effective.

Build and Market a Publishing Identity

One of the hallmarks of book publishing in the last decade—as well as magazine publishing and television programming—has been the increasing pressure to specialize by targeting particular segments of the population rather than a general audience of readers. Small- and medium-sized publishers tend to be specialty publishers almost by definition, staking out an individual niche or a few niches with shared characteristics and overlapping audiences.

The name Random House was derived from the idea that the company would publish a random assortment of titles, both fiction and nonfiction, covering whatever topics interested Bennett Cerf and Donald Klopfer, the company's cofounders. Today this giant house, a conglomeration of imprints that is itself a small piece of an even larger company, still publishes books on a large number of subjects. It also has works in other media. With the advantage of their large resources, such corporate giants can adopt strategies unavailable to the smaller publisher. They can offer seven-figure advances to celebrity authors, and their staff of publicists has daily access to the most widely read magazines and most widely followed talk shows in the country.

Such publishers have the power to move large quantities of books through large-scale expenditures, and while smaller publishers simply can't compete on this field, they fortunately don't have to. The reading public is large enough and diverse enough to absorb everything done by the major houses, including the celebrity books, and still want more. Actually not just more, but different. As a publisher of any size, it's your job to bring authors and readers together. One way to be effective is by learning a subject, knowing the writers prominent in that subject, and cultivating the core audience.

Economies of Scale

Aside from the editorial consideration, from which it helps to know something about the subjects you are publishing, an important reason to specialize as a small publisher is that a lot of marketing, and probably the most effective marketing, is simply too expensive to do with one title. While the corporate giants, banking on the name recognition of a well-known author and assuming large sales, can market at least some of their titles one book at a time, smaller publishers must make their marketing dollars work harder by marketing an entire line with every individual title.

Of course, every book you publish will get the same generic attention any book would get. You send galleys to the prepublication reviewers and to newspapers and magazines. You promote the author to talk shows, or if it's a book of photographs, you try to get the photos serialized in particular magazines. You put it in your catalog, and you show it at the book trade shows. With rare exceptions, you can pursue these avenues with any book on your list, and the costs are relatively predictable. They're within your basic budget.

But what if you want to promote the book through direct mail? What if you want to exhibit the book at a particular professional meeting or a trade show for specialty retailers? You can't set up a direct-mail program for one book, and it's simply too expensive to attend these shows unless you can amortize the cost of your marketing over a number of titles. You need to have a whole line of books you can promote.

DEVELOPING NAME RECOGNITION

The same is true, of course, with your public relations efforts. With a line of books in a particular niche, you can make yourself known to the editors and producers who are interested in your topics. They see you as the resource, which in fact you are. They will take note of each title you publish, and as a result, you will get more and better publicity for each book. You have in effect created marketing value through the identity of your company.

If being a specialty publisher has cachet with the media, the same is even truer for readers and authors. Publishers that have established themselves in a niche can use their position to develop relationships with their audience, becoming the first place for readers to look for further titles. Ask professionals in a particular trade or hobbyists with an unusual interest about who provides their favored resources, and they can often name specific publishers. At the same time librarians and bookstore buyers keep lists of where to find specialty titles and readily recognize the names of small publishers that do quality books in their field. Ask any of these people which major corporate publisher was responsible for a particular celebrity biography, and they wouldn't have the faintest idea.

One further advantage of this strategy is that, as a leading publisher in a small niche, you can attract the leading authors in that niche. If you can't compete in terms of the size of the advance you offer or the status of your name, you can compete by being the best, most active, most visible, or even the most personable publisher within a small field. You have something you can build on and a strategy with which you can build.

BRAND YOUR COMPANY, IMPRINT, OR SERIES

Possibly the hottest concept in publishing today, "branding" is neither new nor the exclusive province of the corporate giants who are leading the current charge toward name recognition for their books. Nevertheless, the remarkable commercial success of IDG's For Dummies® books and their subsequent acquisition of Cliffs Notes™, another publisher with brand name recognition, has led many publishers to take a new look at the advantages of branding for establishing consumer recognition and loyalty to a series, line, or imprint. In the hunt for repeat buyers, publishers are searching out and using household names, strategic alliances, repetitive titles and cover designs, special imprints, logos, and packaging features. John Wiley & Sons demonstrated its enthusiasm for this strategy by buying IDG.

Interestingly enough, IDG's success in branding with their For Dummies books runs counter to most "branding" in book publishing, which usually tries to extend the image of a niche publisher to a related line. Having launched their For Dummies series with computer titles, the original core subject matter of the company, the company aggressively used the look and name of the series to create simple introductory materials on a whole variety of subjects.

More typical of the use of branding in publishing are the Fodor's and Frommer's travel guides. Both publishers offer a series of books that are narrowly focused on travel destinations and consistent in their treatment and packaging. Consumers who buy a Fodor's or Frommer's guide to London know exactly what kind of information they will find in all the other guides.

Here the value of a series overlaps with the value of a brand, but it is interesting to note that even a company like Fodor's seeks to enrich its name. Take for example *Fodor's Golf Digest's Places to Play in the Southeast,* which takes advantage of two brands. Note also that both publishers have several series, each of which is titled with the publisher's name as the first element of the title, like Frommer's Born to Shop books and Fodor's Short Escapes and Citypacks.

Somewhere in between, the niche publisher that tries to establish name recognition for an imprint and the wide-ranging For Dummies titles might fall the example of Dorling-Kindersley and its Eyewitness Books. Having come to publishing through packaging and design, Dorling-Kindersley developed a uniquely appealing, effective, and easily recognizable look to illustrated books. They, too, have branched out in subject matter and format—for instance, the Eyewitness Travel Guides—extending their unique approach to pop-up books, project kits, and software. Nevertheless, all the books are identifiable by the look and feel of the design as well as the distinctive DK logo.

Without getting into the realm of copyright and trademark law, it should be noted that successful branding seems to spawn imitators, so that even when a brand name is protected, competing publishers often follow in the market with knockoffs that, to the undiscerning eye, seem to have much the same appearance and appeal as the branded original. I conclude from this that, while branding offers a wonderful competitive advantage, it provides neither market invulnerability nor product immortality.

PARTNER WITH NONPUBLISHING ORGANIZATIONS

The Jossey-Bass–Drucker Foundation example demonstrates a common pattern in which a publisher combines its business expertise and development capacities with an organization that provides a recognizable name and information base. The relationship, while more complex than the standard author-publisher relationship, nevertheless follows that model.

Other patterns are possible, however. Many nonprofit public service organizations, spiritual groups, and professional organizations have book quality information of potential interest, both to their members and to a wider audience, and they are open to working with publishers in a variety of ways. Some are happy to underwrite all or part of the development costs. Others will commit to purchasing a certain number of books for resale to their members while offering publishers the right to sell the book in all other markets. Still others will look for a copublishing arrangement where they share expenses and want the credit of an imprint to promote the organization. Such deals are available on both small and large scales and can represent a steady stream of income or a one-time infusion.

Angel City Press, a small Southern California-based company, has competed successfully in the highly-competitive, hardcover gift book market by adopting a variety of such strategies. In creating *Monterey Jazz Festival* by William Minor, for instance, the press partnered with the Jazz Festival management and were thus assured that the Festival would purchase books to sell at musical events. Similarly, the *El Cholo Cookbook* by Merrill Shindler was sold at all five of the wildly popular El Cholo restaurants in Los Angeles.

Whether or not such strategies are a realistic possibility for you, they convey a lesson every publisher should bear in mind: When you publish for a known audience, you maximize your chance of success.

Jossey-Bass Partners with the Drucker Foundation

A remarkable instance of branding—and one that offers a clear-cut example of how branding can benefit a publisher—developed through a long-standing alliance between Jossey-Bass, Inc., Publishers, a division of Pearson Education, and the Peter F. Drucker Foundation for Nonprofit Management. As is typical in this kind of relationship, the idea of working together developed slowly and as a result of occasional meetings between representatives of the two institutions.

In 1993, Drucker approached Jossey-Bass with a book proposal for *The Drucker Foundation Self-Assessment Tool*, a workbook and facilitator's guide based on the legendary management guru's own consulting work. To the satisfaction of both parties, the book did spectacularly well, selling about 60,000 copies, in no small part because it carried the Drucker name.

Despite the success of this title, neither Drucker nor Jossey-Bass had immediate plans to follow up with other books. Nevertheless, they stayed in touch, and eventually the idea of an anthology surfaced. The result was *The Leader of the Future,* a compendium of articles that included almost every major name in the management field. While three editors shared credit for the book, the cover carried the Drucker Foundation's name over the title, indicating to readers that Drucker was the ultimate source of the information. This was not simply a marketing ploy, since all royalties due to contributors were actually assigned to the Drucker Foundation.

Not only did the book sell well, but for Jossey-Bass there were collateral advantages. Knowing everyone of significance in the field personally, both foundation president Frances Hesselbein and Peter Drucker himself invited them to contribute to the volume. So Jossey-Bass was now publishing people it could never have afforded to sign up as authors. As a result, the publisher not only saw growing sales, but it was suddenly attracting authors it wouldn't have otherwise signed. The books put Jossey-Bass's name on the map in the business and management market.

Going into this project, both parties also agreed that, if the book were a success, they would look for other topics to do as a series. In fact, the volume landed on *Business Week's* bestseller list (a first for Jossey-Bass), was translated into fourteen languages, and inspired the 1996 launch of a quarterly journal, *Leader to Leader,* and two follow-up volumes, *The Organization of the Future* and *The Community of the Future.* At last count, worldwide sales for all three books stood at around 350,000 copies.

Much of the success of all these projects can be attributed to the importance of the Drucker name. Each volume in the leadership series features a similar design with the name prominently displayed, and the journal is marketed as a cooperative publication from the Drucker Foundation and Jossey-Bass Publishers.

Having experienced these triumphs and attracted a loyal following of readers, Jossey-Bass and the Drucker Foundation are continuing their partnership with the publication of *Leader to*

Leader, a collection of articles that first appeared in the journal of this name and a new *Wisdom to Action* series. All of these accomplishments offer a classic lesson in the value of alliances, the power of a name, and how that power can be extended to the packaging and marketing of specialized information, both in books and journals.

3

Marketing and Sales
in the Book Trade

While a bookstore seems like the most logical place to sell a book, for small, start-up publishers, getting books into bookstores, getting them sold to actual readers, and then getting paid are daunting and often discouraging tasks. The difficulty is rooted partly in the nature of the bookstore, partly in historic trade practices, partly in recent changes in the book industry, and partly in the number of books published annually and the ensuing competition for readers.

Until about twenty years ago, bookstores were mostly mom-and-pop affairs run by people who found pleasure in the business of selling books and made a modest living thereby. Profits were small, and the cost of carrying inventory a stretch, but publishers helped out by allowing the practice of returns. Because most bookstores were tiny by today's standards and carried far fewer titles, a high percentage of their income came from the new hardcover titles. The paperback revolution came along and broadened the book market, but it didn't really change the structure of the industry.

While there were fewer publishers in those days, a greater percentage of ordering was done directly through the publisher rather than through a wholesaler. Publishers' sales reps visited the stores, made suggestions, wrote orders for the new titles, reviewed the publishers' backlists, and even checked the store's shelves to see what the bookseller had in stock. Computerized inventory systems and automatic reordering were yet to be invented. In this now lost and perhaps simpler world, the sales rep acted as the liaison between publisher and bookseller, carrying news and points of view in both directions. Margins, ever tight, favored the publisher, and the publisher held the power to dictate terms.

Into this mix came a myriad of new small publishers, independent distributors, new technology, and the chains. For small publishers during the seventies and eighties, life was good, if not easy. They had to fight for recognition, but there was an expanding market and niches to fill. The new distributors were anxiously seeking publishing clients and could provide a range of valuable services a small publisher might not want to pursue in-house. These services were costly, but there was still a fair amount left over even for titles that sold in small numbers. When, from time to time, a bookstore or even a small chain went under, distributors shielded their publishers from losses. When distributors went under, many of their publisher clients followed.

This period also saw the agglomeration of corporate publishing, the growth of the chains and the decline of the independent bookstore, the establishment of Ingram as the preeminent wholesaler, the trend toward discounting, and, most recently, the emergence of the online bookseller and just-in-time inventory practices. These changes in the structure of the industry, perhaps inevitable in the contemporary world, have had both positive and negative effects on publishers.

Looking at the big picture, book sales have continued to increase modestly—despite the continuing development of new, competing media—and consumers all over the country now have ready access to more books than they ever knew existed. People in most small cities can walk into a chain superstore featuring 100,000 titles or more, while anyone with a computer and modem can access an online book-seller and tap into a database that includes millions of titles. As a publisher or author, you can now rest assured that the reader who is looking for your book will be able to find it. On the downside, with so many competing titles, readers need to be highly motivated in order to select your book from the many choices that present themselves.

A parallel but more significant development affecting the economics of publishing has been the shift in the power to set terms from the hands of publishers to the chains, wholesalers, and online retailers. Publishers have little bargaining power with the few accounts that control such a large percentage of sales, and as a consequence have gradually ceded discount points. At the same time, they have seen returns skyrocket, but the principle stating that a returned book must be in resalable condition to receive credit, while still written in a publisher's terms of sale, has become increasingly difficult if not impossible to enforce. Those who depend on bookstores for the major portion of their sales, therefore, need a higher sales volume to make a book profitable. They also must squeeze more marketing push out of their tighter budgets because of the more competitive marketplace.

So, as a small publisher, what do you do? The following is a description of the conventional trade practices and options for those who are just starting out. Along with this description I offer a few guidelines to help publishers sort out their options and develop strategies for publishing profitably. These will differ, depending on whether the trade represents your primary source of sales or just one piece of a more complex marketing picture, and there is no one right strategy. The trade can be a profitable channel of high volume sales for the right line, yet for many small specialty publishers, the key to profitability will be found in developing multiple sources of income, of which the trade is one.

TRADE DISTRIBUTION

Small publishers seeking trade distribution are usually looking for a whole group of separate functions that are normally bundled under this rubric, including sales representation to bookstores and whole-

salers, order processing, billing, warehousing, fulfillment, and collections. In fact, depending on their size, position in the marketplace,
needs, and attitudes toward outsourcing, you can purchase various
combinations of these services separately or keep them in-house.

The largest publishers—those with sales somewhere above $50
million—often, though not always, perform all these functions
directly with in-house staff. Many midsize publishers, however, will
contract with commissioned sales reps while maintaining all other
functions themselves. Smaller publishers, of course, have fewer
options and lack the economies of scale that make in-house operations
economical. They must learn to work effectively with companies that
provide the services they need. Following are the most common
methods for contracting distribution services. There is no set formula
for determining which will be best for you, and it may be that not all
options are open to you.

FULL-SERVICE DISTRIBUTORS

For many small and even midsize publishers, working with a full-
service distributor offers the easiest and probably most cost-effective
method for providing the entire range of services mentioned above.
Demanding exclusive distribution rights to trade bookstores and the
wholesalers that supply them, these distributors field sales reps (either
salaried or commissioned), maintain warehouses, ship books, collect
payments, and then pay publishers after subtracting fees that range
from 20 to 30 percent of the net receivables on books sold. Payment
is typically ninety days from the sale of books, and distributors usually
hold back a certain percentage for returns as well.

While these fees may seem high, you need to ask yourself what it
would cost for you to perform these functions yourself, how much of
your time and attention would be required if you didn't outsource
them, and if it would even be possible for you to manage them on your
own. You should also be aware that with the growth of small press publishing over the last twenty years, the most established full-service distributors have grown selective. Where they were previously willing to
work with the one- or two-book self-publisher, most are now seeking
publishers that will be around for a while and with whom they can grow.

If your company is relatively new and has only a few titles, you will have to do some work selling a distributor on carrying your line. Most important, of course, will be the quality of the books themselves and their sales potential. Beyond that, a distributor will be interested in seeing a solid business plan and solid marketing plans for the titles. Before most will commit to working with a new publisher, they want to know that they are dealing with a professional operation that understands the challenges of marketing to the trade.

I suggest that, before setting up the relationship, publishers that are considering working with a full-service distributor ask the following questions:

- Will this distributor be successful at selling your books to the chains and independent bookstores? Does the distributor have good relationships with those stores you see as central to your sales strategy? Do your books fit in with the other lines the distributor carries?
- What is the distributor's financial situation? Is there any danger of the distributor going under? As mentioned above, over the years a number of distributors have declared bankruptcy, causing significant losses for their publishers. In many cases, failed distributors have pulled their client publishers down with them. Your due diligence in this area is critical.
- What is the distributor's record for paying on time? While a subset of the question above, late payment may not always be an indicator of imminent bankruptcy but may reflect delayed payments by the distributor's major accounts. Even so, as a publisher, what is your ability to absorb delays?
- Where will you place among the distributor's client publishers? Would you rather be the smallest client of the more prestigious distributor or a large client for a small distributor?
- What is the distributor's record for communicating with its clients? Even more important, does the distributor provide someone with whom you have a comfortable working relationship? Depending on your point of view, it may be either scary or exciting to learn that when contracting with a distributor you are committing to the business equivalent of a marital relationship. Chemistry counts.

- Does the distributor offer marketing feedback? Do they offer co-op funds for trade marketing programs and advertising? Most small publishers can benefit from as much marketing feedback as they can get. A distributor who is sensitive to your publishing goals and at the same time can speak for the marketplace performs a valuable service.
- What will the services cost you? Neither the most nor least important item on this list, the cost of trade distribution is, nevertheless, one of your larger expenses as a publisher. When figuring the cost be sure to add any extra fees a distributor charges for processing returns, catalog placement, trade show display, and so forth.

The most critical and debated distribution function is usually the question of sales representation. Every publisher wants her books to be enthusiastically recommended by salespeople and appropriately advanced to the bookstores, and every small publisher worries that his books will be the last out of the bag. These are legitimate fears. If your distributor carries 150 publishers and is represented by a commissioned rep who carries twenty small to midsize publishers in addition to the distributor's line, your books can, indeed, find themselves at the bottom of a very tall pile.

On the other hand, some of the changes in the marketplace noted above perhaps mitigate this problem. Superstores with just-in-time inventory will, perhaps, order at least a few of the books at the bottom of the distributor's list, while online retailers will list your book right alongside titles from the major publishers. Even more important, however, will be your track record. As you develop an ongoing relationship with a distributor, your line becomes more important to them. They will convey that message to their reps who will respond by pushing your books up on their list.

Following is a list of eight established full-service distributors. To locate others—smaller, newer, or more specialized—I suggest consulting *Literary Market Place*, attending the BookExpo America trade show, or inquiring among fellow publishers. I should also add that before signing with any distributor, you should talk to as many publishers as possible about their experiences with the company you are considering.

- Consortium Book Sales and Distribution, 1045 Westgate Drive, Suite 90, St. Paul, MN 55114; Tel. (612) 221-9035
- Independent Publishers Group, 814 North Franklin Street, Chicago, IL 60610; Tel. (312) 337-0747
- Midpoint Trade Books, Inc., 27 West 20th Street, Suite 1102, New York, NY 10011; Tel. (212) 727-0190
- National Book Network, Inc., 4720 University Way, Lanham, MD 20706; Tel. (301) 459-3366
- Partners Publishers Group, 2325 Jarco Drive, Holt, MI 48842; Tel. (800) 336-3137
- Publishers Group West, 1700 Fourth Street, Berkeley, CA 94710; Tel. (510) 528-1444
- SCB Distributors, 15608 South New Century Drive, Gardena, CA 90248; Tel. (310) 532-9400
- Words Distributing Company, 7900 Edgewater Drive, Oakland, CA 94621; Tel. (510) 632-4700

DISTRIBUTING THROUGH ANOTHER PUBLISHER

A fair number of midsize and large publishers offer distribution services to smaller presses, which on paper, look essentially the same as those provided by the full-service distributors. In general, I recommend that small publishers look at distribution through another publisher when their titles in some way complement the larger publisher's line. For instance, the publisher of this book, Allworth Press, has a number of titles of interest to working artists as well as others in creative professions. Allworth has chosen to work with Watson-Guptill as a distributor because, among other factors, the larger publisher is established in the art-store market and bookstores recognize Watson-Guptill's strength in the arts. Similarly, the travel publisher Globe Pequot distributes books for several smaller travel publishers, including the household name Berlitz.

One factor to keep in mind when considering distribution through a larger publisher is the publisher's level of commitment to the distribution business. Over the years, some of the largest publishers have identified distribution as a profit center and pursued the business vig-orously only to back off later. A problem can also arise if you have one or more titles that compete directly with your distributing publisher. If you are considering distribution through another publisher, you should ask yourself all the questions that pertain to a full-service distributor, and go forward only if you are confident you can both maintain a good long-term relationship.

Working with Commissioned Sales Reps

Those publishers with enough volume to command the attention of buyers, especially at the chains, often exercise the option of selling to bookstores through commissioned reps. Some find it worthwhile to maintain the facilities and back-office staff to do their own ware-housing, fulfillment, and collections, while others will outsource various aspects of these functions.

Some publishers will pursue a variant on this form of business by having a national accounts manager on staff who sells the chains while hiring commissioned sales reps to sell the independents. Other publishers will maintain a combination of staff and commissioned reps, while a few have come to rely on telephone sales to stores in areas of the country where the independents have grown extremely thin.

In all of these arrangements publishers take on both the control and responsibility for getting a whole range of jobs done well, but from a marketing and sales point of view the most important questions regard representation and payment. No longer shielded by a distrib-utor, a smaller publisher must wait in line to get paid and will take the hit directly if an account goes out of business. On the other hand, having removed a layer of intermediaries, publishers may find it easier to get their message through to bookstores and to develop closer rela-tionships with key accounts.

Getting the Most Out of Your Sales Reps

Whether your sales reps work directly for you or your distributor, they represent your frontline eyes and ears on the bookstore trade. And while their job is to sell the books you publish—and that's what they get paid for—their insights and feedback can be tremendously valuable in helping you publish successfully. They know what's out there, what's selling, and what people are looking for. They also know the financial status of the bookstores they visit, and they can keep you informed if you are at risk.

Because their days are spent talking to booksellers and handling the books of so many publishers, most sales reps have both a solid understanding and reliable instincts about what appeals to readers. You should solicit their feedback whenever you can on titles, covers, price, and even contents. In addition, you should keep them informed about important publicity and marketing developments that will affect the sale of a particular title. While most of your contact with your sales reps or your distributor's sales reps will naturally take place at sales conferences and conventions, you should ask each individual about how and under what circumstances they would like to keep in touch. Most are pleased to receive e-mail letters or faxes when you have a publicity appearance that will affect sales. They also want to know immediately if a title is delayed or if the specs have changed, especially if it is something as vital as an ISBN.

SALES CONFERENCES AND SEASONS

By and large, the book trade operates on two seasons—spring, which extends from January through June, and fall, encompassing the months July through December. Over the years, some of the larger publishers and a few distributors have experimented with a third season, winter, which comprises January through March. In this scheme, the spring and summer seasons are April through August, with fall taking the remainder of the months.

Each of these seasons is marked by its own catalog and sales conference where the publisher and/or other staff present the season's titles. This is the moment you place a book in the larger scheme of your list, the distributor's list, and the book trade in general. Of course, as a publisher going into the sales conference you have already decided on the relative importance of each title and have budgeted accordingly, but you make it more or less official when you tell the sales reps where each title belongs on your list.

More important, because the sales conference is the place where you bring your sales and distribution teams together to voice

47

expectations and set goals, it is imperative to properly prepare for this event. You need to have a marketing plan for each title, and you need to be able to summarize this plan in a few minutes for all those attending. You need to give your reps the essence of each book in a phrase and realistically place it in the context of the existing competition.

At the core of your presentation are the editorial fact sheets, also known as the tip sheets, which provide a marketing summary for each title. Ideally, your tip sheet should fit on one side of an 8½" × 11" page and will include a photo of the cover, a handle—a single sentence expressing the essence of the book—a bulleted list of the book's primary features or selling points, a bulleted description of your marketing plan, an author bio, and the publishing specs—price, format, ISBN, number of pages, and trim size.

In addition to the tip sheet, you should assemble sales kits for each title. These are materials your reps can use to sell the book to book-buyers and/or to educate themselves, and they can either be highly elaborate or utterly simple, depending on your budget and the nature of the book. For fiction, it is customary and necessary to provide reading copies to buyers. For illustrated juvenile books, you will need complete folded and gathered signatures (f and g's), and for a high-ticket, illustrated volume you should have a blad (a full-color printed sample usually of four or eight pages) that shows the cover, spine, a sample spread, and the actual trim size.

When presenting your books verbally at sales conferences and before the assembled reps, remember that the reps consider brevity a virtue. They themselves will have perhaps only a minute to present your book to their buyers, and they can neither use nor remember all the things that you value about each title. They need a few succinct points that will stick and that they can repeat. If you have a fun and interesting anecdote—something truly memorable and repeatable—go ahead and use it. Maybe some of your reps will have the opportunity to repeat it when they are presenting the book, or maybe it will help your book stand out. Above all, bear in mind that the reps will be sitting for several days listening to editors or publishers present hundreds of titles one after another. Don't drone on!

CATALOGS AND ORDER FORMS

When making their presentations to bookstores, your sales reps usually sit with the catalog in front of them and go through the books title by title. If you are working through a distributor, your books will be presented in the distributor's catalog. If you are working directly with commissioned reps, then you will need to provide them with a nicely designed, professional-looking catalog for each season.

The standard arrangement for catalogs is to present the frontlist—the forthcoming books for the upcoming season—at the front of the catalog in the order of publication. You can make some slight adjustments to this order and put your most important featured books first, but keeping the chronological order more or less intact will be helpful for the reps and the stores. Frontlist books usually receive either a page spread or full page in a publisher's own catalog—though less space can also be used depending on the size of the catalog and the number of frontlist titles—while a distributor's catalog will frequently assign half, third, or quarter pages to the less commercial titles.

Again, depending on the size of the line, publishers will often describe their backlist at the end of the catalog. This can be as simple as a line listing or can include thumbnail photos and a sentence of descriptive copy. Larger publishers and some distributors will create both frontlist and backlist catalogs.

The other essential tool used by reps is the order form. An afterthought to many publishers, reps use these every day and want them designed for easy use. Reps are gradually switching over to computerized ordering, so the multipart NCR form currently favored will presumably disappear in the next few years. In the meantime, keep in mind that reps would like the frontlist books on your order form to appear in the same order that they appear in the catalog. Backlist titles should appear in alphabetical order by title. Reps also say that they would like publishers to keep the number of categories to a minimum. Remember, they are dealing with a lot of books in a short amount of time. If they have to struggle with filling out difficult and confusing forms, it takes away from the actual time for presenting and discussing the books.

HELPING THE STORES SELL YOUR BOOKS

As noted above, getting your books into the stores can be a Pyrrhic victory if they sit on the shelves and then get returned. In marketing terms, you have created "push," but you also need "pull"—consumers walking into stores and buying your books—thus creating bookstore reorders and long-term success with consumers.

While a number of chapters in this book describe methods for creating pull—through public relations, direct mail, author promotions, and the Internet—there are some specific bookstore tools that can be used effectively for the right books.

SPECIAL PLACEMENT IN BOOKSTORES

Primarily a marketing method and source of income used by the chains, publishers can take advantage of the option to buy into marketing programs that include bookstore "real estate" and certain promotional categories. These may include: endcaps—shelves at the end of aisles that are perpendicular to the main shelves where special selections are featured; shelf-talkers—customized labeling, which draws attention to certain books in a section; or even inclusion in a particular featured section of the store. While these programs are expensive, the costs are somewhat offset by orders of books to fill the purchased positions in the stores. Specialized publishers should note that such programs can be successful for backlist sales of a line or title as well as current frontlist. These programs may also be available on a regional or seasonal basis.

A variant on the bookstore-initiated promotion is the publisher-initiated use of a point-of-purchase display, or "dump." Typically manufactured as either a floor stand or countertop display unit, publishers usually provide dumps free to bookstores and other retailers with the purchase of a minimum number of copies. And while the purchase of a dump filled with books doesn't guarantee the sale of those books or even that the bookstore will use the dump, it does give you an edge. However, publishers that are new to the use of the displays should be aware that, unlike spinner racks used by other kinds of retailers, once the initial stock is sold, dumps are rarely, if ever, restocked with the books intended for them.

BOOKSTORE CATALOGS

Promotional catalogs—either seasonal or thematic—are effective tools for booksellers and participating publishers and are a common promotional device used by the chains and many of the larger independents. Once again, publishers are expected to bear the brunt of promotional costs through catalog or advertising fees. Bookstores give books that are featured in their catalogs special store placement, and bookstore personnel will naturally think of these books first when customers ask for recommendations.

AUTHOR APPEARANCES

A central strategy for big books, as well as those farther down the list, author appearances both attract readers and serve to win the attention of bookstore personnel. The skilled author will not only sell books at the event but will garner the enthusiasm of bookstore personnel. Hometown readings and signings are, of course, even more successful at selling books, while typically attracting an enthusiastic audience of friends and acquaintances.

More than that, bookstores frequented by authors will often continue to feature the book with special placement and recommend it to customers long after the book has disappeared from the shelves of most stores. Authors who have personal relationships with many bookstores can multiply this effect.

It is important, however, for authors of midlist books who are making appearances in distant cities to be aware that they can show up for an appearance and find an empty bookstore. While this is embarrassing for all concerned, those who are gracious in these circumstances can still promote their books. They can develop relationships with the bookstore personnel and also leave some signed copies for the bookstore to display.

CO-OP MARKETING

A common marketing tool, especially among larger publishers, is giving booksellers the opportunity to make use of "co-op" advertising or marketing money for programs that promote both a particular title and the bookstore at the same time. Typically, the money is made available as a percentage of the book's retail value with a cap on the amount that can be used with any single promotion. While originally this money was primarily used for print or radio advertisements—in which a book or books are featured along with the bookstore doing the promotion—it is now also common for this money to be applied to all the different kinds of programs described above.

Sierra Club Takes Aim at the Bestseller List

Every season brings the task of sorting forthcoming titles into *A* and *B* titles and deciding how much of your marketing budget to allot to each book. You have your lead title, and you know you will give this book extra attention, but something in you says that's not enough. A little voice whispers that you have a book with the potential to go way beyond your usual expectations, and you decide to increase your investment—to budget extra time and money to push your lead title over the top.

Such was the response of the marketing staff at Sierra Club Books when they saw *Material World* by Peter Menzel and Charles C. Mann, a collection of photographs and interviews illustrating all the household possessions of families all over the world. This quirky book stood out, and the staff saw great potential in it, deciding to give it more than their usual attention. Here's what they did to put the book on the bestseller list:

1. **Got the attention of buyers with powerful sales kits**
    While the sales kit is the first stop on the way to establishing a book in the minds of buyers, its potential is often neglected by publishers. Sierra Club provided all the standard information—author bios, subrights information, clips of articles, blurbs, a summary of promotional plans for the book—plus a blad that conveyed the quality of the images.

    They then went a step further by having a single, fully bound proof made by hand and arranged to have this copy sent overnight from rep to rep. This unusual step not only signaled to the reps the publisher's commitment to this title, it also gave them the opportunity to see for themselves the quality of the finished work and to share this opportunity with major buyers.

2. **Pushed for a big bookstore buy-in**

With the marked increase in the number of superstores stocking 150,000 titles and just-in-time inventory procedures, it's fairly standard practice for new books to be bought in ones and twos and to be shelved spine-out. Nevertheless, if reps pick up your enthusiasm, they can work for larger buy-ins.

Having met with the reps at the sales conference and expressed its confidence in this book, Sierra Club took the extra step of asking reps to push for the biggest initial buy-ins they could get. More books in the stores means more attention at the store level and perhaps a face-out display. It also means a publisher is willing to face the economic consequences if the books don't sell and a further loss of credibility with buyers in the future. Pushing for a bigger buy-in is a real test of nerves and is not something that should be taken casually. In this case, Sierra Club felt the risk was justified and was fortunate enough to see its strategy pay off.

3. **Bought into wholesaler and retailer promotions**

The chains and the major wholesalers offer plenty of opportunities to spend money to promote particular titles through holiday catalogs, endcaps, and other special promotions. These programs are expensive and usually represent a stretch for the small and medium publisher. They do, however, sell books. You need to be thoughtful and selective if these expenditures are to be cost-effective, but these programs will increase the exposure of your book both to bookstore personnel and consumers.

Sierra Club took part in a number of these programs and also offered co-op advertising funds to retailers. Publishers should note that because both the independents and the chains can take advantage of these funds, by offering co-op you get the opportunity to work with a variety of retailers on a personal basis. Stores promoting your book will also stock more copies.

4. **Invested in a strong public relations campaign**

With a lot of books in the stores as a result of their initial efforts, Sierra Club now had to bring the book to the attention of consumers. They mounted an aggressive public relations campaign—hiring a team of professionals—and did exceedingly well. The book received glowing reviews all over the country, and the authors were widely interviewed, even scoring an appearance on NPR—an unusual occurrence for a book that is primarily photographic. The strong publicity combined with the strong bookstore presence thrust the book onto the bestseller lists, an unfamiliar but rewarding experience for everyone who contributed to making the book a success.

BookExpo America and the Regional Trade Shows

Originally conceived as a trade show where publishers could display their new and forthcoming books to booksellers, BookExpo America (BEA)—formerly the American Booksellers Association Convention—has long been a major event in the publishing year. Featuring publisher display booths; professional meetings; celebrity booksignings; a multitude of authors, agents, and media personnel; and with an annual attendance of around 25,000 people involved in the publishing and bookselling industry, the show has evolved with the times.

Independent booksellers still stroll the aisles and take advantage of show specials to make purchases, but as their number has diminished, publishers have found other reasons to attend. It's an opportunity to make contacts with professional colleagues, meet foreign publishers and sell rights, take a good look at the competition, gauge recent developments in packaging and design, make connections for subsidiary rights, and meet with the many media who attend.

Because presence at BEA is so expensive—booth rental, personnel time, exhibit costs, travel, and lodging—before deciding to attend, you should have a clear sense of what you want to accomplish, and you need to prepare thoroughly. If there are people you want to meet, start making your appointments well in advance. If you're simply there to explore, perhaps you can share a booth. Publishers that work with full-service distributors can, and often do, buy into their distributors' collective booth spaces and take advantage of the distributors' display personnel and services. Remember, too, that a lot of business at BEA is done before and after the show. Sometimes your most important contacts are made standing in line for lunch, on the shuttle bus, or at parties.

Very different in feel and logistics from the BEA, the regional trade shows sponsored by bookseller associations are still very much the province of independent booksellers, sales reps, and local business. Less expensive and far less glitzy, publishers and their reps attend these shows to renew contacts with booksellers and see the proprietors of small stores they would otherwise rarely see. These are, for the most part, grassroots affairs that are especially valuable for publishers that pursue a strategy of working closely with independent booksellers. For regional and specialty publishers, these shows can be a tremendous boost.

Peachpit Press Hones Effective Show Strategies

While most publishers acknowledge the necessity of "showing the flag" at trade shows, professional meetings, and even occasional consumer book fairs, many are clearly ambivalent and, as a result, tend to be haphazard in their planning and efforts. In contrast, Peachpit Press—a division of Addison-Wesley with a publishing focus on computer graphics, multimedia applications, and Web design—spends weeks preparing for each of the many shows the company attends each year.

"We go to meet the public, the industry, and the press," explains Gary-Paul Prince, a senior publicist at Peachpit. "We can create a presence, launch new products, meet the public face to face, create alliances with other companies, and see the competition. Central to all of these is the human element. We make contacts and get reader feedback, but even more important, we uncover opportunities that we are just blind to most of the time."

Here are some strategies for making the most of any show.

Set goals

Before attending a show, you should make a list of goals. Are there specific people it would be helpful to meet? Do you want to set up accounts with wholesalers and retailers? Get reader feedback?

Make media connections? Plan your time at the show and figure out strategies for achieving each one of your goals.

When Peachpit attends the Macworld or Seybold shows, for instance, it gives company representatives a chance to meet executives from major computer companies and software publishers—people who are difficult to reach on the phone. Once you have met someone at a show and shook their hand, they are more likely to return a call.

Work out the logistics

Should you sell books or partner with bookstores that will do the selling for you? How big a booth do you need? How many staff people should attend? Obviously there's no one right answer for any of these questions, but one way to decide is to walk the show as a visitor before committing to a show as an exhibitor.

After all, booth space, staff time, and travel are all expensive, so you want to have a fairly high level of confidence before deciding. If a show seems promising, you can try a small booth. In addition, negotiate for the best location within your price range.

Train staff

Prior to each show, assemble those who will be attending and conduct a training session. Discuss show goals, schedule booth times, and go over all the rules and regulations of the show. The nature of the show will usually determine who will attend, but it's often helpful to have a range of staff members, including editors, publicists, and other marketing personnel.

Get people to your booth

While most publishers are rather passive about getting show attendees to visit their booths, Peachpit works hard to attract attention. They create special show discounts on books, offer books for giveaways and raffle prizes at other booths and, whenever possible, have authors in attendance. "Authors are a great resource," explains Prince. "Often they are in contact with the companies with whom we would like to develop co-marketing arrangements. In addition, at these shows authors get to meet a large number of our staff people they would otherwise never meet."

> Finally, authors attract readers to a booth, and readers give the kind of feedback publishers desperately need. "They tell us what works in our books and what doesn't work," says Prince, "and sometimes they even give us ideas on how to market our books in ways we would never have thought of."

THE INDEPENDENTS, THE CHAINS, AND THE NET

While this chapter opened with some historical background about how the book trade has changed in the last twenty years or so, lurking behind the entire discussion is the fact that changes taking place at this moment are perhaps more momentous than those we have already seen. I mention this here because the goals and methods of trade sales just described may look either inappropriate or antiquated in a very short time.

For the last few years, a major concern has been the decline of the independent bookstore due to the growth of the chains. Now it seems that the remaining independents, as well as the relatively new super-stores, are under pressure from the Internet. Publishers, like those in every business, must be concerned with being profitable today and being prepared for tomorrow's changes. If your strategy as a publisher has been to rely primarily on the independent bookstore, the future must look exceedingly bleak both philosophically and financially.

My point here, and elsewhere throughout this book, is that merely having worked out a method of trade sales and marketing, you haven't "arrived." Long-term success and survival depend on constantly adapting and developing. No doubt there will always be some wonderful independent bookstores, and while chain superstores are a tremendous and growing source of sales, Internet sales are growing even faster. At this point, no one really knows the fate of brick-and-mortar stores.

FOREIGN TRADE SALES

Beyond the borders of the United States lies a large market for English-language books, both among English-speaking nations—Canada, the

United Kingdom, Australia, New Zealand, and South Africa—and throughout Europe and Asia as well, where large numbers of people read English and are in the habit of buying imported books.

Most small and midsize publishers will want to consider either selling rights to companies based in these countries or finding a distributor of imported books in these markets. The decision, in most cases, will depend on the extent of the line, the presence or absence of an appropriate distributor, and the degree of interest for English versions of these titles.

Throughout Europe and Asia, for instance, many buyers of professional, technical, and medical publications are used to buying American or British books and, consequently, there is little market for translation rights. Conversely, many American publishers find that they will do better selling U.K. rights to a British publisher, who will repackage the book to British tastes, than to export and sell their own editions.

Some of the large, full-service trade distributors in the United States now have their own Canadian warehousing, and some have even created relationships with companies in Canada. Hence, publishers that work with these Canadian distributors are already taken care of in this region.

Finally, there are independent distributors in Canada, the United Kingdom, Australia, and New Zealand that function in very similar terms to the full-service U.S. trade distributors. Because of the costs of shipping books overseas and varying exchange rates, margins are squeezed for all concerned. Before signing with anyone, be sure to investigate your options thoroughly.

4

The Library Market and How to Reach It

According to the American Library Association, there are over 120,000 libraries in the United States, including public libraries (about 8,900 systems with almost 16,000 separate locations), school libraries (almost 100,000), academic libraries (over 3,000), and specialized libraries for corporate, legal, medical, and religious institutions (over 10,000). Altogether libraries account for over 10 percent of all book sales in this country, spending about $1.6 billion annually on books and a total of over $3.4 billion on new materials, including books, subscriptions, and the various formats for audio and video products.

This is clearly a market worth attending to, and though you may not know what percentage of your own sales go to libraries—with the numbers masked by wholesaler orders—there is plenty you can do to optimize your success in selling to libraries.

MAKE YOUR BOOKS LIBRARIAN-FRIENDLY

The first step in building your library market is, quite simply, to give librarians what they are looking for—well-written, clear works on subjects of interest to their patrons. Beyond that, librarians focus on the books in their collections as tools. Because part of their job is to answer questions for people and then to point people toward resources that will provide further answers, librarians look for books that help people get to the critical information they seek as easily as possible. They like to see a clear title and subtitle, a well-organized table of contents, and an index. These features recommend themselves to librarians.

Another major concern of libraries is the cost of processing books—that is, getting them on the right shelves with the right catalog numbers. Do everything you can to make that job easier; get a Library of Congress catalog card number (also known as a PCN, pre-assigned card number) and Cataloging in Publication data (CIP) for each book. These numbers are provided by two separate services of the Library of Congress. For information on securing a PCN, write to the Library of Congress, 101 Independence Avenue SE, Washington, DC 20540, or phone (202) 707-6372. For CIP information, write to the Library of Congress, Cataloging in Publication Division, COLL/CIP (4320), Washington, DC 20450-4320.

The Library of Congress posts information about both of these programs on the World Wide Web (*www.lcweb.loc.gov/loc/infopub/*). You can complete your application for the PCN program online.

KEEPING LIBRARIES INFORMED

Librarians make constant use of standard reference works to find books that patrons ask for, and you should be diligent about making sure that your books are listed. Make sure to fill out ABI forms (Advance Book Information) available from ABI Department, R. R. Bowker, 121 Chanlon Road, New Providence, NJ 07974; Tel. (800) 521-8110) so that your books will appear in *Books in Print* and other similar works. There is no charge for this service.

In addition, it is probably worth the small investment to buy space in *Publishers Trade List Annual*, a hardbound collection of publishers' catalogs that is also published by Bowker and is often consulted by librarians.

Librarians also consult the *Small Press Record of Books in Print* (available from Dustbooks, 5218 Scottwood Road, Paradise, CA 95969; Tel. (800) 477-6110; *www.dustbooks.com*).

THE VITAL IMPORTANCE OF REVIEWS

Acquisition librarians are charged with buying the best new books each year and making wise use of their limited budgets. They need to get the books that people ask for and the outstanding books on each subject, and because they often buy books sight unseen, they need help in finding out which books are well written, authoritative, and important. Moreover, it's important for libraries to have new books on their shelves as close to their publication as possible.

To do this job they lean heavily on reviews, especially the prepublication reviews that appear in *Booklist, Kirkus Reviews, Library Journal,* and *Publishers Weekly*. Looking at sales figures, publishers sometimes wonder if their marketing money is producing results, but the results of these reviews visibly add to the bottom line.

All four of the publications just mentioned have strict rules about what they need to see—galleys, publication specifications, catalog copy, or other descriptive information—and lead time to publication date. The latter is especially critical since it takes time to get materials sorted and sent out to reviewers, to get the book reviewed, and then to place the review in the issue that coincides with the publication date. Write or call these publications and ask for their current submission guidelines, and then follow the instructions they send. Also be sure to send these publications your seasonal catalogs indicating your lead titles. While you may not get every book on your list reviewed, by highlighting the most important ones you increase your chances of getting attention for those. Following are some current addresses and phone numbers:

- *Booklist,* American Library Association, 50 E. Huron Street, Chicago, IL 60611; Tel. (312) 944-6780
- *Library Journal,* 249 W. 17th Street, New York, NY 10011; Tel. (212) 463-6819
- *Kirkus Reviews,* 200 Park Avenue S., New York, NY 10003; Tel. (212) 777-4554
- *Publishers Weekly,* 249 W. 17th Street, New York, NY 10011; Tel. (212) 645-0067

In addition to the above, for children's and young adult books you should send galleys to the following:

- *Bulletin of the Center for Children's Books,* University of Illinois Press, 1325 South Oak Street, Champaign, IL 61820; Tel. (217) 333-0950
- *Horn Book Magazine,* 11 Beacon Street, Suite 1000, Boston, MA 02108-3718; Tel. (617) 227-1555

While all the magazines named above ask for galleys in advance of publication, a review journal aimed at academic libraries, *Choice,* asks for bound books. Contact them at *Choice,* 100 Riverview Center, Middletown, CT 06457; Tel. (203) 347-6933.

OTHER INFLUENCES ON LIBRARY BUYING DECISIONS

In addition to the prepublication journals, librarians often consider newspaper and magazine reviews in making buying decisions. Every good review helps and can be used when promoting to libraries. Still in a class by itself, however, is the *New York Times Book Review* (229 W. 43rd Street, New York, NY 10036; Tel. (212) 556-1234). Whether its influence is based on tradition, status, circulation, or quality, no other newspaper in the country produces as many sales or generates further reviews elsewhere as the *New York Times.*

Finally, many libraries subscribe to book clubs, including some of the smaller, more specialized book clubs, or use book club lists as selection tools. Obviously, trying to sell to libraries by making a book club sale is a somewhat roundabout strategy, but knowing that libraries are motivated by book club sales does provide extra incentive to work with the clubs. It also means that when marketing to libraries, you should be sure to let them know about any book club adoptions.

LIBRARY DISTRIBUTORS

While some of the largest publishers field sales reps who call on acquisition librarians, smaller publishers do have the option of using the services of one or more distributors with commissioned reps. Providing a specialized service, Quality Books, Unique Books, and Superior

Books are each dedicated to filling various niches in library collections with books from the small independent presses who publish in those niches.

For small publishers without an active library marketing program, these distributors offer the potential of incremental sales into an untapped market. However, for publishers already reaching what has traditionally been a market with comfortable margins, the advantages are less clear. Working on a consignment basis, these distributors take hefty discounts. Given the trade-offs, my suggestion is to carefully evaluate your company's total volume, the percent of the total that goes to the library market, and the money and energy you will put into this market. There may or may not be a role for library distributors in your marketing plan.

Quality Books, which is the oldest and largest (founded in 1964, with annual sales near $10 million), serves publishers of every size— from large companies such as Macmillan General Reference, NTC, and Sterling to one-book self-publishers. Quality Books handles adult nonfiction, some children's books, audio, and "nontheatrical" video. Its twenty-two commissioned sales reps sit down with librarians and present from 1,500 to 3,000 new titles during each visit. For sales materials, they carry covers and data slips with bar codes and bibliographic information. They also carry computers with printers, so they can print out information for librarians, e-mail orders directly, or print out a customized order form for the librarian to review and send in later.

To maintain an up-to-date and active list, Quality constantly reviews new titles for its program. Of the approximately 1,000 to 2,500 new books it receives each month, Quality takes on about 20 percent of those submitted. Each book is considered individually by a review committee—including three staff librarians—that uses the following criteria:

- Does this book break new ground or fill a gap on the shelf? If Quality already has several titles on a particular subject, it hesitates to take on another.
- Is the book new? Quality prefers to have information on the book ninety days before publication. It definitely won't consider titles that have already been seen by the library market.

- Is the book well organized? Quality Books tries to apply the same criteria in choosing the books it carries as librarians do in the books they buy.

For further information about Quality Books and its services, contact Quality Books, Inc., 1003 W. Pines Road, Oregon, IL 61061-9680; Tel. (800) 323-4241; *www. quality-books.com.*

While Quality Books is the best known of the library distributors, fielding a national sales force of commissioned reps, it is not your only choice, nor does it require exclusivity. Some publishers combine the services of two or more of these distributors.

Similar to Quality Books in the services it offers, Unique Books is reportedly in a "growth mode." Founded in 1986, Unique carries nonfiction books as well as audio and video titles from three thousand publishers. It fields twenty commissioned sales reps. For further information, contact Unique Books, 5010 Kemper Avenue, St. Louis, MO 63139; Tel. (800) 533-5446; *www.uniquebooksinc.com.*

Founded in 1980, Superior Books represents eighty-five publishers and looks for entire lines rather than individual titles. About half of its twenty thousand titles are children's books. The company will only consider publishers with at least fifty titles. For further information, contact Superior Books, P.O. Box 1371, Bowling Green, KY 42102-1371; Tel. (270) 781-9946.

LIBRARY WHOLESALERS

The American Library Association estimates that two-thirds to three-quarters of all library book purchases are made through wholesalers. Following is a partial list of wholesalers that do a large library business and provide specialized services—bindings, labels, theft detection, and so forth—for libraries:

- Baker & Taylor (the largest supplier of libraries in the United States), 50 Kirby Avenue, Somerville, NJ 08876; Tel. (908) 722-8000; *www.baker-taylor.com*
- Blackwell North America U.S. (international wholesaler of academic books), 6024 S.W. Jean Road, Building G, Lake Oswego, OR 97035; Tel. (800) 547-6426; *www.blackwell.com*

- Booksource (specializes in audio, video, CD-ROMs), OMG Booksource USA, 6122 Reisterstown Road, Baltimore, MD 21215; Tel. (800) 229-2114; *www.omgsic.com/bkshome*
- Brodart Company, 500 Arch Street, Williamsport, PA 17705; Tel. (800) 233-8467; *www.brodart.com*
- Emery-Pratt Company, 1966 West Main Street, Owosso, MI 48867-1397; Tel. (517) 723-5291; *www.emery-pratt.com*
- Ingram Book Company, 1 Ingram Boulevard, LaVergne, TN 37086; Tel. (800) 937-8100; *www.ingrambook.com*
- Midwest Library Service, 11443 Saint Charles Rock Road, Bridgeton, MO 63044; Tel. (800) 325-8833 or (314) 739-3100; *www.midwestls.com*
- Yankee Book Peddler, 999 Maple Street, Contoocook, NH 03229; Tel. (800) 258-3774; *www.ybp.com*

These and other smaller wholesalers provide a host of valuable services to librarians, including the opportunity to reduce paperwork by combining orders from many different publishers, the convenience of online ordering, standing order plans, special binding and processing services, and the advantage of better discounts.

From the publisher's point of view, these wholesalers are often no more than passive order-takers. In the best circumstances, however, wholesalers can provide valuable marketing opportunities for the right book or line of books. Baker & Taylor, the giant in this field, offers everything from print advertising and telemarketing opportunities to distributing advance reading copies. These programs are expensive and appropriate only in certain circumstances.

If the library market is important to you, make the effort to contact representatives of library wholesalers and keep in touch with them. At the very least, make sure to send your catalogs and keep the wholesalers updated on the status of your titles. The bottom line here is to provide wholesalers with complete accurate information on each title so they can, in turn, inform their library accounts and fulfill orders.

If you regularly revise books and bring out new editions, these present opportunities for developing standard order plans. You should inform wholesalers and librarians. In some cases librarians rely on their wholesalers to create and stock core collections. If your titles make it onto such lists, the benefits are solid. When you have the definitive book on a subject or an important reference work, library wholesalers need to know.

LIBRARY MEETINGS

The American Library Association conducts two major professional meetings each year. The summer conference is larger and usually takes place in late June. The midwinter conference usually takes place in late January. Both conferences are heavily attended and offer opportunities to exhibit.

Nevertheless, you should be aware that these are not events at which you will write orders, but places to build awareness of your company and your titles among a group of people who buy a lot of books. You can make personal contacts with acquisition librarians and build a list of names for follow-up. You can also get an immense amount of information on what librarians are looking for and how your books meet their needs.

In addition to these two national conferences, most state chapters also schedule conferences with exhibiting opportunities. Publishers with regional titles may want to consider attending some of these as well as the conferences of the largest states. Dates and locations of the conferences may be obtained from the American Library Association, 50 E. Huron Street, Chicago, IL 60611; Tel. (312) 944-6780. Their Web site has this information and a host of other valuable features; look them up at *www.ala.org*.

DIRECT MAIL

As a group and as individuals, librarians are probably the most diligent and earnest people with whom you will ever work. Their jobs are dedicated to helping people find information, and they value the written word. I've been told by librarians that they read every piece of information that publishers send. How they are able to keep up is beyond me, but to publishers, such statements indicate the value of informing librarians about books through direct mail.

Target the Acquisition Librarian

Your goal should be to build a house list of acquisition librarians who recognize the name of your company and want to be informed about your books. As this list grows, be sure to follow through by sending these librarians seasonal catalog mailings and, when appropriate, special book announcements.

Of course, building such a list takes years, and it requires the internal systems for maintaining and updating the information. A practical alternative for many publishers is to rent lists. There are several sources for such lists, and you can select various parameters when you order, including purchasing budgets, size of collection, and type of library. As with any direct-mail program, it's important to have an appropriate budget and specific goals before you begin. (See more about general principles of direct mail in chapter 6.)

When looking for lists, you can begin with those rented by the American Library Association itself. Phone (312) 280-2460 or write to the address mentioned on page 66. Other sources of lists include:

- Cahner's/Bowker Direct Mail Service, 245 W. 17th Street, New York, NY 10017; Tel. (212) 337-7164 or (800) 537-7930
- CMG Information Service, 187 Ballardvale Street, Wilmington, MA 01887; Tel. (800) 677-7959
- Educational Directories, Inc., P.O. Box 199, Mt. Prospect, IL 60056-0199; Tel. (708) 459-0605
- Market Data Retrieval, 16 Progress Dr., Shelton, CT 06484; Tel. (203) 926-4800 or (800) 243-5538
- Quality Education Data, 1600 Broadway, Twelfth Floor, Denver, CO 80202-4912; Tel. (800) 525-5811 or (303) 860-1832
- School Market Research Institute, P.O. Box 10, Haddam, CT 06438; Tel. (800) 838-3444

What to Send

Publishers often send their seasonal catalogs to libraries, and librarians like to see these. It gives them the opportunity to stay well informed, and it makes more sense than creating an entirely new piece just for libraries. If you can afford to do a little customizing on your catalog, a good strategy is to create a special letter for librarians highlighting areas of special interest. Such a letter can appear inside the front cover or can be an extra bound-in piece with an order form.

But whether you send your catalog or some other kind of brochure, be sure your piece includes all the elements a catalog should contain: a well-written description of the book, biographical information about the author including her qualifications and the titles of previous books or articles, quotes from reviews, and all the pertinent stats—price, trim size, ISBN, LC number, and so forth. Be sure to mention if the book contains CIP information, an index, charts, illustrations, or tables. Reproducing the table of contents—not a standard procedure in book catalogs—can be effective for librarians.

ADVERTISING

Though expensive and often inefficient, there is a role for a thoughtful advertising strategy in a library marketing program. To be effective, however, you need to have a clear message, and you need to integrate that message into your entire library marketing program. An occasional ad, generated out of enthusiasm for a particular book, is unlikely to produce results.

Advertising can be used to position your company, to reinforce your direct-mail campaigns and trade show attendance, and to announce special programs, new lines, and lead titles. As noted above, librarians are serious about buying books with solid information as well as the books their patrons have requested. They are unlikely to be swayed in their buying decisions by expensive or extensive advertising. With this perspective, advertising becomes a tool for informing librarians about what you have to offer.

Keep in mind, too, that because advertising is read with less attention and less credibility, it is most effective as a reminder. There is an advertising adage that you need to hear about something three times before you remember it or act on it. As a publisher, this does not mean that you should run every ad three times. It does mean that when librarians have received your catalog, seen your ad, and visited your booth at the ALA convention, they are more likely to remember your books when ordering.

Practically speaking, if you are trying to build awareness among public librarians, the two magazines you will want to consider advertising in are *Booklist* and *Library Journal*. If you have a strong market in academic libraries, you might also look at advertising in *Choice*.

AUTHOR APPEARANCES

Public libraries throughout the country are working hard to make themselves community resources and not just a collection of books. They sponsor and host events of all kinds, including workshops, classes, and readings. And while library visits and events traditionally have not been included in author tours or public relations plans, these events can be rewarding for the author who has the energy and enthusiasm to make libraries a part of her promotional work. Pursued with diligence, they can build an audience for a book through word of mouth and create sales.

While a library might not increase their stock of a particular title just because an author does an event, librarians do recommend books to patrons, and a long waiting list at the library will induce at least a few anxious readers to visit their local bookstore for a copy. Though books usually are not sold at library events, authors can distribute flyers with coupons for direct sales through the publisher. It's also common for authors to stock books of their own, and they can create a flyer for taking their own direct orders.

A parallel strategy is to approach the local "friends of the library" to sell books, offering the group a discount and thereby turning the event into a library fundraiser. This is a win-win situation. The results may not be as dramatic as Oprah's efforts, but librarians and their patrons are, after all, a dedicated audience for books. Savvy authors and publishers will cultivate and support them.

5

Selling Direct

$\mathbf{M}$ost large, general trade publishing houses don't want to be bothered with selling single copies of books directly to consumers, and perhaps this approach makes sense for them. Targeting anonymous consumers rather than a specific market, they're not cultivating repeat buyers for a particular line or subject matter, building lists of buyers, or developing new books for the buyers of previous ones.

In contrast, when publishers' businesses are based on repeat customers—scientific, technical, and professional publishers accustomed to selling via direct mail, and niche publishers targeting a tightly focused market—they know that it's worth their while to cultivate every direct channel possible. They want to develop and maintain close relationships with their buyers, and they see subsequent sales as the natural outgrowth of these relationships. If you share these aims, here are some techniques you can use as part of a comprehensive marketing strategy that cultivates direct sales.

READER RESPONSE CARDS

Called "blow-in" cards because they are inserted by air pressure into a bound book, reader response postcards are an easy and inexpensive way to build a mailing list and cultivate reader feedback. Typically used by niche publishers, these cards usually offer the reader the opportunity to receive a free catalog, updates on time-sensitive information, and information on related books or products via a self-addressed, business reply postcard.

If your books are truly of interest to a specialized audience, the readers of your books probably want to know about your other books. They will send these postcards in, and they will give you valuable feedback, if you ask them for it. They will tell you what books they want (an unscientific yet useful way to do market research) and tell you what they liked or didn't like about the book at hand. You won't agree with everything they tell you, and it won't all be accurate, but you can learn a tremendous amount from your readers if you have a way of asking them.

If you do decide to use blow-in cards, here are some general principles to observe: First, provide the postage. Presumably, you will make money dealing with customers who actually ask for your sales materials, so you want to do everything you can to make it easy for them to respond. Don't make them go looking for a stamp. Second, make sure that you provide enough space for them to write their names legibly, and ask them to print. Third, if you have more than one line of books, or if you occupy more than one niche, code the cards so you know what materials to send.

BACK-OF-BOOK CATALOGS

As a niche or specialty publisher, every time you sell a book you should be selling your whole line of books, and one effective way to do this is by placing a catalog at the back of every book. You can include either a full or partial catalog, simply listing titles or describing the books at length. You can feature other books by the same author and other books that treat the same subject. In general, I recommend providing customized, descriptive copy. As a book-buying consumer myself, an alphabetized list of titles without further copy strikes me as close to use-less. Even if I already know the authors and the books, I'm not sure how I will use this information when I see it at the back of the book. On the other hand, if I am interested enough to look over the back-of-book catalog, and if, having read the book, I want more, then I am a serious, qualified buyer for the titles I see listed. Give me enough sales copy so that I can actually decide, Yes, I want the book described here.

Having provided the copy, you now, as publisher, have several options. You can simply hope that I will go to the bookstore and pur-chase the book (if it happens to be in stock), you can sell it to me right now, or you can give me the option of getting more information. If you are set up to take and fill individual orders, provide as many ordering vehicles as you can, including a detachable order form, a toll-free phone number, a toll-free fax number, a Web site, and an e-mail address. If you would rather refer sales to bookstores, or if your line of books is too large and the titles too complicated to expect to make a one-step direct sale, you can offer readers the opportunity to request your catalog.

A word about bookstore relations here: Over the years, book-stores—especially independents—have been vocal in expressing their distress with publishers that compete for their customers, and they have been especially grieved by seeing discounted offers for books from publishers within the books they are selling. If you have a strategy of selling direct as well as through bookstores, you may want to discount titles under certain circumstances, but you should be cau-tious about implementing this strategy at the bookstores' expense. If your back-of-book catalog offers to sell the book at hand at a dis-count, why should a reader buy it in a bookstore, and why should booksellers stock it? If, on the other hand, your catalog offers a variety of titles that won't usually be stocked in bookstores, and offers them at full price, you have satisfied the bookseller's legitimate com-plaints. This seems fair to the store, since you are probably selling backlist items that won't usually be in stock; fair to the customer, who is gaining the convenience of a direct order from the home or office; and fair to you, the publisher, who has made the sale and gained a competitive edge against other books on the subject by cultivating a direct customer.

BACK-OF-ROOM SALES

For certain books and certain authors, the sales made at or through speaking engagements can represent a huge percentage of the total sales of a book. I know authors who have self-published and sold a huge number of books this way and others, especially consultants and independent contractors, for whom book sales represent an insignificant portion of their income but an important way to promote further speaking engagements and jobs.

Publishers and authors who foresee that back-of-room sales will play an important part in the sales of their books would do well to look at their respective roles in this strategy while negotiating their contracts. Publishers can encourage authors to inventory and sell their own books by offering an extra discount on the purchase of significant quantities, and they can provide flyers or some other kind of sales material to authors. In addition, authors can sometimes arrange to have their publisher drop-ship orders for them.

The range of events at which authors can sell their own books is as varied as the books themselves. There are, of course, the myriad business lunch meetings with featured speakers that take place every working day of the year in every city of the country. There are also church events, public lectures, adult education classes in public high schools and libraries, workshops and demonstrations in retail outlets and hobby shops, arts and crafts fairs, PTA meetings, and more.

Being an author automatically qualifies a person as a presenter at such events. It doesn't, however, make a person a good speaker or a good salesperson, and these are both critical qualities for success on the "rubber-chicken circuit." Naturally, having the right combination of information and audience will be an important factor in making sales, but being a dynamic speaker is often a greater factor. So those who want to pursue this avenue but lack speaking skills would do well to get some training.

The second factor, being prepared to sell books, is simpler to arrange. When possible, speakers should have an assistant at a table with books, receipts, and a cash box for making change. Above all, make it easy for people to buy. Round off prices if you can, and offer some kind of discount. There is no time like the present for making a sale. Give people an incentive to act now, but if for some reason they hesitate, be sure to have flyers with coupons for people to take home with them. You may not get a lot of these back, but what you get is extra cash in the pocket.

BOOK FAIRS, TRADE SHOWS, AND CONVENTIONS

There are, of course, a lot of reasons for attending these kinds of events, such as recruiting new authors, finding new wholesale and retail outlets, learning about current issues in a field, creating institutional partners, or simply selling books. The relative priority of these goals will depend on the nature of your publishing program, how long you have been in business, how well known you are to your target audience, and the nature of the event itself.

A book fair attended by the general public is best suited for selling books and getting your name out, whereas a professional meeting may be the opportunity to cultivate relationships and find new authors. Your priorities and the nature of the event will also determine who on the publisher's staff will attend. For many publishers, sending acquisitions editors to professional meetings is standard practice. In the same way, academic presses often have a person in charge of text and supplementary-text marketing who routinely attends events in specific academic areas. In contrast, consumer book fairs are usually staffed by customer service reps and salespeople, whose primary duties at these events are to sell books, hand out catalogs, and assist authors during their presentations. I know of several publishers that have found book fairs to be a great way to sell returned and damaged books. Not only have they cleared away dead inventory, but they have been known to make money doing so.

THE AUTHOR AS FEATURED SPEAKER

While, for the most part, authors are on their own in setting up speaking engagements and selling their own books at these events, book fairs, conventions, and professional meetings offer excellent opportunities for authors and publishers to work together. A publisher that takes exhibit space can stock books by featured speakers and arrange for author signings at its booth. This is clearly rewarding for the author, and it draws a lot of attention to a publisher that might easily be neglected in the flurry of activity that usually surrounds such events. Having an author in attendance will also boost sales at the booth for all of the publisher's titles.

SPENDING TO BE NOTICED

Because book sales rarely cover the expenses of attending and staffing an event, you need to be clear that the event will serve your long-term marketing goals before you decide to attend. If, for instance, you want to be recognized as a publishing resource by a certain group of professionals, you know that your presence at their professional meeting will contribute to this goal and to the profitability of your company.

If your goal is not only to be recognized, but to be seen as a major presence in the industry, you may also want to take a more active role in the organization and the event. There are often volunteer opportunities for associate members, whatever they may be called—a role usually fulfilled by the publisher—as well as sponsorship opportunities for conferences, receptions, dinners, or parties. The money invested here is akin to advertising. You are creating a position and an identity in the minds of your target audience. If you have the capital and the margin to do this, it can work heavily in your favor.

DIRECT MAIL

In the world of marketing, where the unsubstantiated and unprovable often hide behind the mysteries of art and intuition, direct mail stands out as a device akin to a science—being measurable and repeatable—and a remarkably effective way to sell books, at least certain books. A brief introduction to the basics of direct mail as they apply to book marketing follows here and in the next chapter.

WHAT ARE THE RIGHT BOOKS FOR DIRECT MAIL?

With a highly targeted readership, direct mail has traditionally played a central role in the marketing of academic, scientific, technical, and professional books. The potential buyers of these books are easily identifiable. They belong to professional associations, read certain journals, and attend specific conferences. They can be found relatively easily, and they will be responsive to the publisher that presents a line of books in their area of interest.

These same principles apply to readers with very specialized interests—model railroaders, weavers, fine woodworkers, political activists devoted to a particular cause, or members of small or sectarian religious groups. Because their interests fall outside of the mainstream, the books that would interest people in each of these cases are not likely to be stocked in the bookstore, yet because of their affiliations, the people themselves can be found rather easily.

Other books that rely successfully on direct mail include directories, series, annuals, and reference books. Since the buyers of these books usually have a clear idea of the contents, having used earlier editions or similar volumes, they have a high degree of confidence in the books offered without having seen them. They are looking for current information, and they know the nature of the resources they are purchasing. Even where the particular title is new to them, the nature of the information included in a particular volume can be clearly and effectively described and defined in a brochure.

THE BOOK CLUB MODEL

What then about trade books, literary fiction, general nonfiction, biography, humor, and history? What about all those books that we buy in bookstores? Can't they be sold through direct mail, too? In fact, they are, and in large numbers by such large book clubs as the Book of the Month Club, Literary Guild, and the Quality Paperback Book Club. Well established in consumers' minds, these clubs are successful for a number of reasons. They offer their customers value through discounts and premiums on popular books, they command adequate margins through their buying practices, and they not only cultivate, but demand customer loyalty through the use of the negative option—"Unless we hear from you, we will send you this month's selection." In a sense, these clubs are the ultimate purveyors of convenience. They make a selection on your behalf, and they send it to you without you lifting a finger. If you give them your credit card number to keep on file—an option they offer—you don't even have to think about paying them. They take care of it for you.

Despite the popularity and success of these clubs, when you look over a comprehensive list of book clubs serving the public, you will notice that beyond the few largest clubs that appeal across a broad range of readers, most are focused on a particular interest, hobby, or profession. These clubs adopt some of the strategies of the three general clubs listed above and some of the strategies of a niche publisher selling direct. They target a segmented group with books that will be of interest to that group, plus they offer all the conveniences of buying direct from a service-oriented club.

THE VALUE OF EXCLUSIVITY

One of the clichés of direct-mail marketing is that the best products to sell direct are those that are sold exclusively this way. The reasons are fairly obvious. If I want to buy a book, and I can go to the bookstore and get it today instead of having to wait, that's an advantage. If I can save the shipping and handling charge by buying from a retailer, that is an advantage, too. Or, if I want a book on a particular subject, but I don't know which title will best suit my needs, I appreciate being able to examine the bookstore's selection. I can thumb through each book, read a few pages, and choose the one that addresses my interests most thoroughly or most succinctly—whichever is of most concern to me.

On the other hand, as a book publishing and marketing professional, I know even the largest bookstores won't have on their shelves some of the public relations directories mentioned in the bibliography of this book. If I want to buy one of these, I will have to get it directly from the publisher. So when the publisher's brochure arrives, I ask myself only one question: Do I want to buy this book or not? The questions, Where will I buy it? and How much will I pay for it at one outlet versus another? don't arise.

This is also the case with scientific, technical, and professional books—the kinds of books most commonly sold through direct mail. Since these are usually handled by only a very few specialized bookshops, publishers offer their titles through the mail with relative, if not complete, exclusivity.

THE VALUE OF CONVENIENCE

In an earlier era, when a large percentage of the U.S. population was scattered in rural areas and without easy access to retailers with a broad spectrum of goods, people got in the habit of ordering what they wanted from major retail catalogs such as Sears Roebuck and Montgomery Ward. Today, though the percentage of the population without ready access to large retailers is relatively small, there are still people who prefer the convenience of buying direct. And while direct mail now competes with television, the phone, and the Internet for soliciting and making direct sales, it continues to offer publishers an effective method for reaching certain kinds of buyers, and it offers readers a convenient way to buy certain books.

The element of convenience plays a critical part in the design of an effective direct-mail package. From the outset, however, it is important to keep in mind that, in presenting your potential buyers with a direct-mail offer, you are offering not only a product, but a convenient way to buy that product. You should be clear that part of what you are selling is convenience itself.

THE INTERNET

While total book sales continue to increase modestly in the United States, recent industry statistics indicate a decline in direct-mail sales. And while bare statistics don't provide causes, there is no doubt that this decline can be explained by the migration of buyers to the Internet.

If direct mail was successful in the past partly because of the convenience it offered, readers who spend the day at their computers find the Internet an even more convenient place to make their purchases. There are few books that can't be found quickly and easily, so exclusivity is rarely an issue. At the same time, both retailers and publishers are quickly learning to offer readers the information they need online to make a buying decision.

Both direct-mail sales and Internet sales are discussed below, in chapters 6 and 7, respectively. By way of introduction to these discussions, however, I would like to emphasize that the methods described are not exclusive. Your direct-mail marketing can and should offer e-mail as an ordering option and your Web site as a source of further information. In the future, direct mail may, in fact, increasingly represent the first step in a two-step sale that involves referring the buyer to a publisher's, retailer's, or book club's Web site.

6

Direct Marketing in the Internet Age

S ince the first edition of this book, the growth of Internet sales and the consequent migration of orders to online booksellers such as Amazon.com and BarnesandNoble.com has had a profound impact on the direct-mail portion of publishing. Publishers who previously rejoiced in the kind of quantifiable results described later in this chapter ("I mailed x number of pieces and got y number of orders back") must now look more closely at the total sales produced by the pieces they put in the mail, their own Internet sales, and sales made through retailers. Though direct-response rates have fallen off, this doesn't mean direct-mail marketing is ineffective. It means you must employ more sophisticated methods for measuring the results.

Publishers who used to run "direct-mail programs" are now reshaping them in name and substance as direct marketing programs. The new name not only reflects a greater emphasis on marketing over sales, but that the program encompasses e-mail and Web site marketing as well as regular mail. While much of what follows addresses direct-mail as opposed to e-mail, most of the principles will, nevertheless, apply. In addition, I do discuss e-mail newsletters as a marketing tool in chapter 7.

THE ECHO HAS GOTTEN LOUDER

In the first edition of this book, I discussed what used to be called "the echo effect," sales generated from direct mail through other channels. I noted that these were hard to trace, harder to quantify, and inappropriate as a justification for spending money. My concern was for publishers who lost money because they failed to set strict goals and maintain the discipline of analyzing the results of each direct-mail campaign.

With the public now at home ordering online, however, this picture has changed. People may read through your direct-mail piece, ignore the order form and go to their computers, so even when orders don't come via your mailed order form, they may be generated by your mail. The important thing to keep in mind is that Internet retailing is passive, relying on buyers to seek out the book they want. In contrast, direct mail and/or direct e-mail generates buyer response. There's a symbiotic relationship, so the results of your efforts through mail and e-commerce need to be considered together.

The experience of Pfeiffer UK, a firm devoted to business and management resource materials, offers a perfect example. A few years ago the company saw a decline in responses to its catalog mailings and decided to eliminate these efforts. The results? The phone stopped ringing and a very successful line of products stopped moving. Though it wasn't getting catalog order forms, the mailings were clearly generating phone calls to customer service and online orders. Soon thereafter, the company revived the mailings and sales returned.

This, then, is the new paradigm. When measuring the results of your direct marketing beyond the clearly traceable orders, you have to calculate as best as you can the number of orders the program generates through other outlets, whether your own customer service, brick-and-mortar stores or online retailers.

THE NEED FOR DISCIPLINE

The most consistent and serious error I encounter among publishers that are interested in the possibilities of direct mail is thinking of this technique as something to be tried on an occasional basis for an occasional book. This is a method, or rather a lack of method, doomed to failure. Direct marketing makes money as a program, not as a one-shot event, and its effectiveness comes from building up a customer base that will buy repeatedly. This is vital, whether you are selling clothing through a major catalog or books to a narrow audience.

So, to publishers that are considering direct mail as a marketing method, my first question is: Do you have systems in place to track orders and capture the source of your sales? In other words, after you have done a mailing and sold some books, can you add the names of those who ordered to your database, and will you be able to retrieve those names and mail to them again? If you can't answer yes but are still interested, your first step is to set up the systems necessary to capture this information.

This is something you can do either in-house or outsource. There are companies that will take orders for you, process the billing, ship the books, capture the mailing codes, and maintain your mailing list. You can also contract for any combination of these services. While outsourcing tends to be expensive, the relative economy of using such services will depend on a number of factors, including your overhead, the size of your direct marketing program, the cost of hiring and training new employees, and whether or not you will need to install or upgrade new computer equipment.

THE NUMBERS TELL A STORY

Figuring the profitability of a direct-mail campaign used to be one of the most reassuring and predictable activities in any publisher's marketing department. You could determine to the dollar the profitability of your program. You knew how much you spent and you how much you took in, so you could create a profit-and-loss statement for each mailing as well as for the entire program. You knew how many pieces you mailed and how many orders you got, so you could easily figure the response rate of your mailing efforts. You knew the total dollar amount of these sales, so you could figure your average order size, and you could compare the results of different mailings, offers, and lists. Even better, you could learn from both your successes and failures and apply what you had learned.

If your books are not available through retailers or other outlets, you can still generate this level of accuracy in your reports. If not, you will have to project some kind of baseline sales and then consider any additional sales, not just those that come directly to you, as the result of your direct marketing efforts. This extra step, and the fuzziness of the baseline that you must assume, is unfortunately a given in the current marketplace.

Acknowledging that fact, you can still come up with some pretty accurate estimates of the profitability your program. Here is a basic format, which you can customize to fit your circumstances for figuring your profit or loss for each mailing:

Profit-and-Loss Worksheet for Direct-Mail Promotions

Revenues

Gross sales	=	$
– Returns	=	$
Net sales	=	$

Expenses

Cost of goods	=	$
Fulfillment costs 　(includes order processing, shipping, 　customer service, credit card 　processing, etc.)	=	$
Cost of processing returns	=	$
Bad debt	=	$
Premium (if applicable)	=	$
Cost of promotion 　(printing, postage, mailing services, 　list rental, etc.)	=	$
Overhead 　(including fixed costs of the promotion, 　independent contractor's fees, 　and staff time)	=	$
Total expenses	=	$

Profit/(Loss)

Net sales	=	$
–Total expenses	=	$
Profit/(loss)	=	$

Looking over this worksheet will give you a good sense of the clarity that you can achieve in determining your costs and your profits. Once you have a sense of the precision by which a direct-mail promotion can be measured, the next thing you will want is the ability to look at your assumptions and project your break-even points. You want to know how much you can spend and still expect to make money.

For the purpose of projecting these factors, as well as for analyzing the results, you should set up a spreadsheet that looks something like the one below. Using a spreadsheet such as this, you can easily chart the interaction of critical variables—costs, response rates, order size— on the profitability of particular mailings and on your program as a whole. Note that for the sake of simplicity I have figured the cost of goods at 15 percent of the sales price and have omitted calculations on either charges or expenses for shipping and handling.

Spreadsheet Model Projections for a Direct-Mail Program

House List	# Mail	Avg. Order	Response Rate	$ Total Revenue	$ Total COG	$ Promo Cost	$ Profit/ (loss)	ROI %
List A	10,000	$25	8%	$20,000	$3,000	$8,000	$9,000	112%
List B	10,000	$30	5%	$15,000	$2,250	$8,000	$4,750	59%
List C	5,000	$32	2.5%	$4,000	$600	$4,500	($1,100)	–24%
List D	5,000	$36	2%	$3,600	$540	$3,000	$60	2%
List E	10,000	$30	1.5%	$4,500	$675	$8,800	($4,975)	–57%
List F	10,000	$36	3%	$10,800	$1,620	$8,800	$380	4%

While the numbers above are entirely fictitious, they illustrate an important point—namely, that direct mail makes sense as a way to reach a stable group of customers on a repeated basis—in other words, the house list. When you rent new lists, you are not only looking for incremental sales, but you are seeking to add new buyers to your own list. When you break even with a rented list but add hundreds of names to your house list, you have created equity. People who have bought from you once and like the books they have bought are likely to buy from you again, and at a higher rate than any other group of prospective customers.

A second important point illustrated by this spreadsheet is how hard it is to make money on direct mail with low-priced books. With a projected response rate of 2 percent on List D, I had to assume an average order size of $36 and promotional costs of 60¢ per piece to come out slightly ahead. In fact, it is extremely difficult to do any but the simplest mailings for 60¢, and a 2 percent response rate on a rented list would be considered very good in most instances. You need either high-priced books or a line that can generate sales of several titles per order.

The Joy of Testing

If you offer readers a 20 percent discount on your book or books, will you pick up enough extra orders to make up for the difference in price? If you offer a money-back guarantee, will you be flooded with returns, or will your extra sales more than make up the difference? Will you attract more readers by emphasizing the how-to elements in a book or its well-researched information?

The joy of direct mail is that you can actually get exact numerical answers to these questions. You can test every element in a direct-mail campaign, and the next time you mail you can repeat the strategies that worked and abandon those that didn't. The one principle to keep in mind is that you can only test one thing at a time. If you want to test different versions of your cover letter, you must test them on the same list, and the list must be divided equally. You can't mail one version of the letter to New York and another to California and be assured of accurate results. You have to use what is called an A/B split. The list must be divided so that every other name falls on each list. In the same way, if you want to compare the relative value of two lists, you must send the exact same packages to the addresses of both lists on the same day.

Renting and Cultivating Lists

Marketers often say that the three main elements in a direct-mail campaign are the list, the offer, and the package, and that of these, the most important is the list. You can have the greatest offer in the world, the most spectacularly designed package, and an excellent product, but if you mail to someone who isn't interested, your efforts will go to waste.

In one sense, the entire basis for a direct-mail program is the list itself. You may have great books on a topic of special interest to particular readers, but if you don't have, can't create, or can't find a list that targets those readers, you don't have the makings of a direct-mail campaign. Conversely, if your books are of general interest to a general audience, your audience will be too diffuse to reach profitably through direct mail. In designing a direct-mail program, you have to begin by asking yourself: Can I create, find, or rent lists of people who will want to buy my books?

The Care and Feeding of Your House List

At the core of every direct-mail program are your own past customers. If your publishing program is focused on a particular niche, then those who have bought a book from you before are probably interested in your other books and will buy again. In the best of worlds, you would be publishing enough books to justify getting back to these people on at least a quarterly basis. You want to maintain continuity with your buyers, remind them of what you have to offer, and reinforce their interest. If possible, you would like them to think of your publishing program as the solution to their professional needs or as a wonderful resource for an interest or hobby.

If you see direct mail as a key element of your marketing program, then building your house list must also be a daily activity. You can collect names at shows and conventions, insert reader response cards in your books, and have your authors refer readers to you through flyers and/or a toll-free phone number.

You can also look upon mailing to rented lists as an investment you make in acquiring new customers. Returning for a moment to the

"Spreadsheet Model Projections" presented earlier in this chapter, we notice that two rented lists (D and F) made barely any money, while two others (C and E) actually lost money. Were these mailings a complete loss? The answer is not as simple as it appears, but depends on the future sales that come from the new customers acquired as a result of these mailings.

Following the model in this spreadsheet, we see that by renting four lists we have added 675 customers to our database at a cost of $5,635 (the total loss we incurred over the four mailings). If, however, over the next year, we mail to these new customers four times and get an 8 percent response rate on each mailing with an average order of $25 (the response rate and order size of House List A), we have almost made back our loss. In the second year, even with a declining response rate, we begin to make money.

Such a program still might not represent a very efficient use of our money, but again, these numbers are theoretical. If we can avoid the debacle of List E, either by offering higher-priced books or by mailing only to those lists where we can expect a somewhat higher response rate, the program becomes profitable more quickly. Moreover, if our customers continue to buy from us for many years, then the investment we have made in this program has contributed to building a solid foundation for a direct-mail business.

Another important element of a direct-mail program is good customer service. You need to provide your potential buyers with confidence that they are dealing with a reliable firm, even though they can't see you, and you have to be efficient at responding to their needs. Every time you get an inquiry, that person should be entered on the mailing list. While not everyone who inquires will buy, the percentage who actually become customers will probably be higher than names you acquire by other means. You need to set up a system to track the source of inquiries—whether through ads, postcards, conventions, or author appearances—so you can increase your efforts to generate yet more inquiries, and you need to mail to inquirers in a timely way. Through careful tracking procedures you can determine how many inquirers actually turn into customers, and how many times you should mail to people before dropping them from your list.

This leads to one of the basic principles of maintaining a direct-mail program: Keep your list clean. The first step is to get addresses updated by requesting address corrections from the post office. You also need to keep track of the last date that each customer placed an order so you can calculate a customer's response rate in relation to the date of her last order. As with other kinds of businesses, some customers tend to return and buy on a regular basis. Others will buy from you occasionally. Still others will buy from you only once. By creating a field in your database for "date of last order," you can determine at what point—six months, a year, two years, five years—it becomes unprofitable to mail to a former customer or inquirer.

Acquired Lists

Because a major contributor to success in direct mail is the ability to target your audience as precisely as possible, seeking out appropriate lists is a central element in every direct-mail program. Whether you are publishing books on model railroading or organizational development, your job is to find lists of people with a demonstrated interest in the particular subject matter. If you are new to the process, be aware that while there are available mailing lists that represent every imaginable interest, not all of them are created equally.

As a general rule, the best lists are those made up of recent direct-mail buyers and, for your purposes, direct-mail bookbuyers in particular. Less responsive, but still good, are subscribers of magazines or journals in your subject area. These people have presumably demonstrated their responsiveness to direct-mail buying by placing an order for a subscription, and they have qualified themselves by subject matter. Association member lists follow these for demonstrating an active interest in your subject area, but they usually won't get as high a response rate, simply because the people on these lists have shown less commitment to or comfort with buying by mail.

At the bottom of your choices are compiled lists or, more specifically, "lifestyle" lists. These lists have been put together from a variety of sources—phone directories, product registration cards, demographic surveys, public records, and so forth. While much cheaper on a per-name basis, I would counsel publishers to avoid these lists completely. Response rates to compiled lists are too small for publishers to make money.

If you are new to direct mail, you can begin your research process by looking at the *Direct Marketing List Source* from Standard Rate and Data Service. This annual resource describes mailing lists and gives their sources and costs. You can also contact local list brokers, talk to them about your project, and get their suggestions. A knowledgeable list broker can be helpful, but you need to be careful in taking their advice, since they won't know your business as well as you do, and they may be more concerned with making a sale than with your profitability. Once you have built your house list to an adequate size, you can also talk to list brokers about renting your list. In this way your list not only becomes part of the equity of your business, but adds to your income.

Trading Lists

For publishers that find themselves more collegial than competitive with other publishers sharing their niche, sharing and exchanging lists can be an excellent option for all parties. In such a situation you know you are getting names of highly qualified leads, and you are reducing your mailing costs at least by the cost of the list rental. Customers who are seriously interested in hard-to-find books and information are also well served by such an arrangement.

Testing Lists

Among the advantages of scale gained by publishers that build up large direct-mail programs is the ability to test lists. For instance, if in your research you find six lists that you consider to have good potential, and each has tens of thousands of names, you can run a test in which you take five thousand names from each. You ask for an "nth" select—n representing the fraction of names you select from the entire list—and the names are systematically pulled to insure against bias. After you see how each list performs, you can then mail to the remaining names on just those lists that were profitable. Returning again to the spreadsheet above, we can see that we actually made money on Lists D and F. If there are another hundred thousand names on each of those lists, we can go ahead and mail to these people with a high degree of assurance that our mailings will be profitable.

Merging and Purging

As a kind of footnote here, because large numbers of people appear on many mailing lists, you must make the effort to avoid sending them duplicate mailings. To address this problem, mail houses perform an operation known as merge/purge. On their computers they merge the various databases of your house and rented lists, and they discard (i.e., purge) duplicate names. Besides saving money on postage (those duplicate mailings can add up!), another effect of this merging is that instead of doing multiple mailings you are doing only one mailing. With a greater number of recipients in your mailing, you can sometimes move into a higher level of sorting for postal purposes and qualify for greater discounts.

Piggyback Mailings

An option offered by some trade organizations, piggyback mailings combine materials from several publishers into one mailing. Sometimes participating publishers will take orders individually, and sometimes the organization sponsoring the mailing will collect payment and fulfill orders for all the participating publishers. The cost of such promotions is considerably less than doing your own direct mail, but because the presentation is usually so diffuse, it's hard to come out ahead on these. They don't substitute for an effective direct-mail program, but if you don't have a line that is either large enough or focused enough to justify building your own direct-mail program, you might consider experimenting with these. One word of caution: Be sure that the mailing is adequately focused and targeted to those with a high degree of interest in your book or books. As with all direct mail, the name of the game is finding an audience focused enough to get a profitable response rate.

MAKE THE BEST OFFER YOU CAN

You've found some potential buyers and put your message in their hands. What kind of deal do you give them? What do you do to get them to actually place the order?

One of the clichés of direct mail is that you have to give people a reason to buy direct. As we noted, if the only place they can buy something is directly from you, this is an obvious incentive. Naturally, you want to emphasize this point with a graphically bold statement that says something like: ONLY AVAILABLE DIRECT FROM THE PUBLISHER— NOT SOLD IN BOOKSTORES.

In addition, or in most cases, instead, you want to create an offer that makes people feel like this is not only something they want, but this is a deal so good that they can't pass it up. One of my all-time favorites appeared on the outer envelope of a mailing from the Quality Paperback Book Club. It reads:

> 3 BOOKS, 3 BUCKS
> NO COMMITMENT. NO KIDDING.

Not only is the offer clear and catchy, there's an obvious bargain. Beyond that, the club makes a major point of telling you that, unlike other offers you may have received, you really are not required to buy anything more. In this they have overcome a major obstacle for potential buyers. As a publisher, you should note that since the Quality Paperback Book Club will continue to send their mailings with the negative option, it is confident (and presumably has the experience to prove it) that it will make money on the "no commitment" offer. As a reader, however, you're not concerned with its profits, but with the deal you are getting, and it is a good one.

Compare this offer to one made by the History Book Club:

> CHOOSE ANY 3 BOOKS FOR ONLY $1 EACH,
> PLUS A 4TH AT 35% OFF THE PUBLISHER'S PRICE,
> WITH NO OBLIGATION TO BUY MORE.

This is still a good deal, and the History Book Club, also sensitive to the issue of commitment, scores the same point as the Quality Paperback Book Club. Nevertheless, as a reader, I have to stop and think about the overall offer and calculate what it's worth. I think about the 35 percent discount and the price of the fourth book, and when I try to amortize the cost over all four books, I get confused in the process. As a marketer and copywriter, the last thing I want to do is confuse my potential customers. Not having participated in these campaigns, I don't have the statistical results. I do know, however, that as a potential buyer I'm much more likely to respond to the simplicity of Quality's offer.

MAKE YOUR OFFER TIMELY

One of the things your offer needs to do is to get people to act now—now meaning absolutely this minute—rather than put your direct-mail package aside in the "think about later" pile. It's true that a few orders from your direct-mail package will arrive in your mailbox months and even years later. Most, however, come in the first three weeks. Given that it is so easy to put off doing something and then just drop it, you want to get your potential customer to take action immediately.

You can offer a prepublication discount that expires on the publication date, an inventory reduction sale with an end date, or a Christmas sale. Here's an offer I received from Cornell University Press:

OVER 500 BOOKS! EXTRAORDINARY SAVINGS! LIMITED TIME OFFER!
OUR FIRST SALE IN FIVE YEARS!
ORDER NOW! SALE ENDS JUNE 15

I didn't buy any books from this catalog, but I was impressed with the way they combined a sale expiration date with the notice that this was their first sale in five years. As a potential customer, I knew that if there was anything I wanted, I could get it at a special bargain price that wouldn't be repeated soon.

SELL THE BENEFITS

Advertising copywriters distinguish between the features and the benefits of any product they are selling, and they explain that their job is to emphasize the benefits. I interpret this distinction by saying that the features of a book are all the things that make it good. The stunning prose style, clear and concise explanations, sinuous plot, profound theory, detailed information, and stunning illustrations—these all contribute to your enjoyment. But you read a book because you want to be moved to the depths of your soul, to become enlightened, to be improved as a human being, or to become more effective at your job. You want to win friends and influence people, have thin thighs, save the earth, or do it yourself and save money. These are benefits.

In fact, among all these benefits, probably the most effective in any direct-mail copy is the offer of wealth or, almost as good, the opportunity to save money. Note that both of the book-club ads quoted above offer financial bargains. Also perennially effective in direct mail is use of the word "free." Buy a book and you will get something else—another book perhaps—"free." You don't buy two at half price; you buy one and get one free. It's an offer that's hard to resist. Or, you buy this book and get a special report or an update free. It's a bargain. Ad people say that "free" is the most powerful word in the English language. It certainly pulls its weight in direct mail.

Here are a few more sell lines that I have culled from my mail over the years that display the selling power of financial benefits:

- HOW TO BE 15%–20% RICHER BY ELECTION DAY
- WOULD YOU LIKE TO RECEIVE FREE CLIP ART SOFTWARE?
- HOW TO SELL AT PRICES HIGHER THAN YOUR COMPETITORS

It's hard to answer "No, I don't want it," to any of these, and that's precisely the point.

Even when your primary benefits appeal to the mind and spirit, it doesn't hurt to give people a bargain. A letter from Smithsonian reads, "You're invited to experience one of the most rewarding and exciting enrichment programs in the nation today . . . at a special introductory price." Similarly, the History Book Club, which attracted my attention by offering a good deal on the outer envelope, follows up in their letter with an appeal to my intellectual curiosity and suggests that good books for people of my caliber are hard to find. They, however, can solve this problem, and in this suggestion capture the value of exclusivity, even if only by implication and not by fact. Their letter begins:

Dear Reader,
If you love to read history, you know the problem. Good history
books are hard to find. Few bookstores offer you a satisfying

selection—either in terms of quantity or quality. Often the books they do carry tend to be sensational, not substantial.

Offering value, intellectual satisfaction, access to worthy books, and convenience, this club package offers a model of how to highlight benefits.

MAKE IT EASY TO ORDER

Having put together an appealing direct-mail offer, your next job is to make it as easy as possible for the recipient to buy. This means offering as many response vehicles as you can. Provide an order form and business reply envelope with prepaid postage. Give toll-free phone and fax numbers. Provide an e-mail address and a secure Web site.

In addition, you should offer as many payment options as possible, including all major credit cards. Offering a "bill me" option will increase your response rate, but you will have some uncollectable debt. Most publishers still come out ahead offering this payment option despite the nonpayers.

OFFER THE BEST GUARANTEE YOU CAN

Over the years, direct-mail companies have overcome consumers' resistance to buying direct by featuring responsive customer service and excellent guarantees. You should do the same. The J. Peterman Company catalog says, "Absolute Satisfaction. Anything less, and you get your money back." This definitely increases my confidence in placing an order. Similarly, at the front of its catalog, Nolo Press prominently places its "no-hassle guarantee," which reads, "You can return anything you buy directly from Nolo Press for any reason and we'll cheerfully refund your purchase price. No ifs, ands, or buts."

The Smithsonian mailing quoted earlier includes this guarantee as part of its order form:

I accept your invitation to become a member of the Smithsonian National Associates for the next year for only $10. That's HALF the regular annual dues.

I understand I am entitled to all benefits mentioned in your letter including twelve issues of SMITHSONIAN magazine. If I don't agree my membership benefits are worth twice the price, I'll tell you so and owe nothing.

Offers and guarantees such as these are all effective at increasing the response rate. Of course, no matter how good your books, you will get some returns, some from customers who were truly dissatisfied, some from people who misunderstood what it was they were ordering, and a few from individuals who are willfully abusing your goodwill. Be that as it may, offering and standing by a strong guarantee will contribute to your efforts to build a responsive direct-mail list.

CHOOSING THE RIGHT PACKAGE

Direct-mail packages can vary tremendously in cost and complexity. You can put together an oversized, four-color, multi-insert piece—complete with novelty devices such as stickers, stamps, or tiny pencils—or you can send something as simple as a postcard. The most appropriate option in any particular instance will depend on several factors.

Since print runs are an important factor in determining your printing costs, the size of your program will, to a certain extent, determine how simple or complex your package will be. A second determining factor is the nature of the books themselves. From the buyer's point of view, the piece you mail represents the books featured in the mailing. You need to represent your books appropriately in your mailing pieces. If you are selling lavish coffee-table gift books, you need a brochure that recreates some of that lavish feel. If you are selling comprehensive reference works, you won't need fancy color work, but you do need to convey in one way or another the extent of the material in the books. Finally, your package will reflect its immediate function. If you are trying to make a sale to a new customer, you need to provide all the information that person will need to make an informed decision. On the other hand, if you are simply reminding an annual directory buyer that a new edition is now available, you can often do that with a minimum of descriptive copy.

THE FIVE-PART MAILER

The most common format in direct mail, and this applies to books as well as other products, consists of five pieces: an outer envelope, a letter, a brochure, an order form, and a return envelope. This may or may not be the most cost-effective package for your program, but this style of package has evolved out of a long history of testing. In general, it has been shown that each of these pieces, while adding to the cost of a mailing, also increases the response rate.

The Letter

Testing has also shown that the letter is the most important element in this package for making the sale. It's the first thing read, and, if effective, it will be read from beginning to end. This is where you tell readers how they will benefit from your books, and like the History Book Club letter quoted before, this is where you appeal to their needs and desires. Your letter should direct the reader to the brochure and order form, provide a postscript with some kind of incentive for immediate action, and include a boxed notice or headline at the top of the letter. Each of these elements improves response rates.

The Brochure

Although brochures may vary considerably in size, design, and expense, there are certain essential elements that should always be included: thorough, descriptive copy of your books with bullet points, a photo of the cover, and the basic stats such as price, trim size, number of pages, and ISBN. Your copy should highlight any special features that will make the book useful or valuable to your intended reader such as original research, lavish photographs, or the inclusion of a glossary and bibliography.

Academic, technical, and professional publishers often include the full table of contents in their brochures, as these reflect the range of material covered in a work. If you have testimonial or review quotes, this is where they will appear. In addition, make sure that your ordering information appears on the brochure in case it gets separated from the order form. Also, recipients will sometimes pass on a flyer to a friend or colleague, or they might want to place a second order themselves. In either case, you want to make it easy for them to order despite their lack of return envelope or order form.

The Outer Envelope

In recent years I have received quite a few direct-mail packages in envelopes that imitate or suggest either checks, bills, or governmental communications. I am relieved to report that none of these have come from book publishers.

Though I am offended by this approach, I do recognize that the use of this strategy conveys an important message to all direct mailers. You need to get people to open the envelope. You can do this by making the package look like something it isn't—a personal letter or a tax refund—or you can put a message on the envelope designed to attract, intrigue, or excite the recipient. For your most loyal customers, your return address on the envelope may be enough. For new prospects, however, there should be something on the envelope to make them want more. Use a headline with a special offer. Trumpet the benefits of a book or books. Announce a premium.

The Order Form and Return Envelope

Constructing a good order form can be an amazingly laborious process. I suggest collecting samples of well-designed forms and using them as models when constructing your own. Your main concern is to have an easily understandable form that leads the buyer to insert all the information you need. If you use a window envelope, you can have the mailing label as part of the order form. This insures preservation of your mailing codes as well as accurate shipping information. Be sure the form includes your address and toll-free numbers (in case it gets separated from the return envelope), special offers and terms, payment and billing options, shipping and handling charges, and all applicable taxes.

Packages mailed in a number ten outer envelope often contain a number nine business reply envelope and an order form that fits into this envelope. Whether you adopt this format or not, the point is to make ordering as easy as possible.

SELF-MAILERS

The self-mailed catalog is a mainstay of direct-mail marketing because it works. People who are accustomed to buying direct don't need to be led by the hand. They receive a catalog and simply say, is there anything in here that I want? They look at the pictures and read the copy looking for those items that are of interest. The "sell" is in the range of items, in the items themselves, and to a lesser extent, in the copy. Special offers and pricing are also influences in the buying decision, but the reason catalogs are effective is because they're direct, easy to use, and familiar.

If you have the right line of books and the right audience to rely on a catalog, here are a few basic points to keep in mind. First, use the cover effectively. Use a prominent headline to announce a special offer or highlight your most important new book. Second, use a publisher's letter on the inside front cover to address your readers personally and direct them to the items you think will sell the best. You can also use this letter to discuss your special offers and invite feedback. Finally, if your catalog is lengthy and likely to remain as a reference on the shelf of your buyer, be sure to include an index or table of contents. Your order form should observe the principles enumerated above. In addition, you should include a return envelope that is easy to use and easy to remove.

DON'T SURRENDER YOUR CUSTOMERS

As important as direct mail may be in generating sales, it's perhaps even more important for building customer loyalty. Don't give up your customers, either to online booksellers or your competitors. Once your customers go elsewhere to purchase, they are open to purchasing whatever books may be offered, and those books won't necessarily be yours.

Create policies to keep these customers as your own. Plaster your 800 number and Web site on every page of your direct-mail package. More important, make an offer with a real incentive to buy directly from you. While you may not want to undercut bookstore retailers or compete with Amazon.com by giving discounts, you can give your customers something in return for placing their order through you. A free subscription to a newsletter, updates, a special report, free shipping: it's not so important what it is, as long as the offer sounds attractive.

More than anything, take advantage of the Internet yourself. Be sure to ask your customers for their e-mail addresses (so you can e-mail offers to them) and steer them to your Web site. Once you are able to track electronic orders, you will probably find that the decline in response to your direct mail is less than you thought.

7

Marketing and Sales
on the Internet

Annual Internet book sales, well over $600 million in 1998, were projected to surpass $2 billion in the year 2002. While some of this growth presumably represented new business, a large portion was displaced from other sources, particularly "brick-and-mortar" retailers, book clubs, and direct mail. With such a large sector of the marketplace informing itself and buying online, it is absolutely imperative for publishers—whether trade, academic, or professional—to aggressively cultivate new and existing avenues for online marketing, publicity, and sales. At the same time, the Internet offers a large number of low-budget promotional opportunities for authors willing to make the effort.

WORKING WITH ONLINE RETAILERS

As with other facets of the publishing and bookselling industry, online retailing is clearly dominated by two giants, Amazon.com and

BarnesandNoble.com. And while the other retail giant, Borders, along with numerous independents, have mounted online bookstores attempting to compete in this market, the lion's share of sales are, at the moment, made by Amazon.com and BarnesandNoble.com.

There is, of course, no reason to limit your online promotions to the largest retailers, and it's entirely possible that—with the speed of change in online business—by the time you read this, the relative strength of these online retailers may have changed. Nevertheless, the two largest retailers are offering the most sophisticated and powerful marketing opportunities for publishers, and these serve as a model for the increasingly important world of the virtual bookstore. If you have good relationships with independent bookstores, you should certainly encourage them to develop comparable marketing opportunities on their own Web sites and provide any help you can.

Your Internet marketing and sales efforts should begin by creating relationships with the people at the online bookstores who will be dealing directly with your company. At the largest sites, this means the tech people and the category editors. For independent bookstores, this usually means the webmaster.

A good place to start is by sending online booksellers electronic versions of book covers, catalog copy, tables of contents, endorsements, flaps, and panel copy. Nevertheless, because the major virtual bookstores are overwhelmed with their rapid expansion, you will need to be proactive to make sure all your material gets posted. Contact the tech people and work out methods for transferring this information electronically so that you can get information to them in as timely a manner as possible.

Just as it does in a conventional bookstore, the cover helps to sell the book online, so you need to do the work to get the cover posted. In addition, the more information you can provide, the better your chance of making a sale. Online buyers like as much information as a buyer in bookstore, so try to emulate the bookstore experience by providing the kind of information buyers get when they pick up the book.

In addition to individual listings by title for each book, online booksellers have locations on their sites that highlight bestsellers, category favorites, seasonal titles, and new titles. There are special listings for award winners, Oprah's picks, and specially recommended titles. Web sites feature titles on their home pages, offer staff reviews, highlight titles on the opening pages of specific categories, and send subscribers e-mail newsletters featuring selected titles in categories of interest to readers.

Treat the category editors for these sites as both catalog buyers and media contacts. Provide them with advance reading copies, covers, and press kits, and work as closely as possible with them. After all, their job is to promote books, so by providing them with adequate information you increase the chance your books will be highlighted in one of their site's many valuable locations. Once again, if you do get a review, either online or on the virtual bookstore's site, you will sell many more books if the cover and your copy have been posted.

HarperSanFrancisco reports that the day after a title received a prepublication review on the front page of Amazon.com's Religion and Spirituality category, sales of the book jumped into Amazon's top fifty. The book was included in the category e-mail newsletter and then highlighted on Amazon's bestseller page—and orders came flooding in for a book that wasn't yet available. These results were not the result of marketing muscle, but simple diligence in making sure category editors got the appropriate materials for a book that could stand on its own.

CREATING YOUR OWN WEB SITE

Whatever the size or nature of your publishing company, it's now as essential to have your own Web site as a telephone or fax machine. For a huge number of people, especially the educated book market, the Internet has become a ready source of information, and for many the first place to look for reference materials or tools. Whether you're a niche publisher with a targeted audience or a general trade publisher working in a variety of areas, your readers and potential readers are on the Internet. You need to meet them there through an actively maintained, interesting Web site that invites the involvement of both your established audience and potential new buyers.

Use Your Web Site to Convey Your Identity

While you may be publishing text-heavy books designed for a technical audience, when designing your Web site, keep in mind that your presentation will live in the highly graphic environment of the Internet. This doesn't mean you must suddenly invest in eye-popping animated graphics. It does mean you should devote some energy to creating an attractive, clear, interesting presentation. Also keep in mind that though you are publishing books, which by definition are static, Internet users are accessing your Web site through the interactive medium of their computers.

In other words, an effective Web site is not simply an online catalog, brochure, or billboard. You need to use the capacities of the medium as thoroughly as you can while conveying who you are and what you have to offer readers. Of course, the design and implementation of your Web site can be expensive, depending on the size and complexity of your site and the options you utilize. On the other hand, if you have the time and inclination, you can use simple off-the-shelf Web authoring tools and spend next to nothing on design.

However you choose to handle the technical aspects, you should try to integrate the design of your Web site with the style and appearance of your books, your catalog design, and your logo and, thus, reinforce the graphic identity of your company. Every site needs a focus, so unless you have a different site for every book, the focus needs to be your identity as a publisher. This doesn't mean you have to put your mission statement on the front page of your site, but rather that every page of the site should reflect and embody that statement.

For a niche publisher this is relatively simple, since everything in the site will be related by content. Those who publish in more than one area will have to rely more heavily on other unifying elements and implement a branching structure to lead visitors to the area that interests them.

Provide Visitors with Valuable Information

While some visitors to a publisher's Web site are there to buy a book, others are there to explore an area of interest. If they have come to the site through a thematic link, then they may not even be looking for a book, though they may want to know something contained in your books. Or maybe they have accessed your site directly to learn more about a particular title. Perhaps one of your titles has led them to investigate your entire line. You don't want to disappoint any of these people. Your site should be set up to answer their questions as well as feed their desire to buy and read what you have to offer.

What should your site include? Simply put, as much as possible— covers, catalog copy, tables of contents, reviews and testimonial quotes, author bios, and sample chapters. Hopefully you will have all these materials for every book in your line, both frontlist and backlist. Here's a place you can continue selling titles no longer stocked in bookstores.

Once you have posted your basic book information, you should try to add some depth to the site. Ideally, you want to make the site a source of news so people will return from time to time. You can feature new and forthcoming titles, and provide information about author tours and speaking engagements.

You can also take another, broader approach to making your site a newsworthy stop on the Internet by becoming a clearing- house for information related to your books. A chess publisher, for instance, might post tournament schedules and results. Similarly, the publisher of books on environmental policy can post original or reprinted environmentally-related articles, or information about bills pending in Congress with an environmental impact. Instead of your Web site being one big advertisement, you're now the chief advertiser on a Web site that has some of the qualities of a newsletter or magazine. You offer readers a reason to return on a regular basis, knowing that a certain percentage will be moved to buy, and you establish yourself as a primary source of valuable information on a certain topic or topics.

USE YOUR SITE TO BUILD RELATIONSHIPS

In addition to providing information, you should make every effort to take advantage of the Internet's interactive capacities. Consider creating interactive events with your authors, online chat sessions, or e-mail correspondence. You might also want to poll your Web site visitors about what kinds of books they are looking for and ask them for feedback on books they have read. Be prepared, however, to respond to their comments. This, too, is time-consuming, but it's a valuable investment. Once you engage your readers and potential buyers in a dialogue, they will become your loyal customers. Your Web site offers you the opportunity—even if only in the virtual world—to hand-sell your own books, and you shouldn't pass it up.

GETTING PEOPLE TO VISIT YOUR SITE

Once your site is up and running, make sure you notify all the major search engines about the content, so you will be listed when people do a search on your topic. Also, be sure to use the meta-tag feature—hidden text within site headers—to make sure the key words that are central to your topics show up in searches.

In your explorations of the Web, you will undoubtedly discover sites with contents complementary to your own. Be sure to set up mutual links if they are amenable. You want to make it as easy as possible for people to find you.

SELLING BOOKS DIRECTLY FROM YOUR WEB SITE

Whether or not you sell direct from your site will depend on your larger strategy regarding direct sales. If, like many large publishers, your strategy is to move high volume through the book trade, you may not want to compete with your retailers. At the same time you may not be set up to process direct orders efficiently. Many small publishers, however, welcome the opportunity to make sales at either full price or a small discount and will want to turn their Web sites into sales outlets. Even those who are cautious about competing with their regular retail accounts can offer special prices on backlist items whose sales have slowed to a trickle or offer prepublication specials to a loyal group of customers and site visitors.

If your line is large enough and you expect to make steady sales through your Web site, you will want to offer your customers the comfort of "secure transactions" and the handy device of a virtual shopping cart. Like other Internet services, you can outsource these options or develop them on your own server. If you are just starting out and don't want to invest in these services immediately, you can offer Web visitors the option of phoning your toll-free number or e-mailing in credit card orders.

Stone Bridge Press, a small publisher with a specialty in Japanese language and culture, supplements its income and attracts visitors to its site by also acting as a retailer for third party Kanji and language software programs. Since Stone Bridge is not the publisher of this software, but only one of many retailers, they feel free to price these products aggressively. Having the software available on the site has increased their visibility among the prime audience for their books, contributed to the bottom line, and helped to develop alliances with other companies serving the same market.

SELLING DOWNLOADS

While the idea of replacing printed books and journals with their online equivalent has been widely discussed in the last few years, implementation up to this point has lagged, presumably because readers still want lengthy materials in printed form. Still, there are indications that interest in directly accessible, text-based materials is slowly increasing, and there is no doubt that at least some consumers already prefer purchasing written information online in electronic formats rather than in printed books.

Software publishers routinely sell and download programs through the Internet, and users have slowly been conditioned to accept accompanying manuals in electronic form, accessing them and printing them as needed. In a parallel development, academic publishers are posting journals online and making them password accessible to subscribers who are already receiving them in conventional print form. Presumably, though not necessarily, this represents the first step in the process of withdrawing the printed format completely.

PinkMonkey Sells Downloads to College Students

A relatively new Web-based business, PinkMonkey.com (*www.pinkmonkey.com*), is now selling downloadable Literature Notes—study guides similar to the well-known Cliffs Notes, Test Preparation

---

Guides, and Course Guides—which offer "concise reviews of intro-ductory level course work such as Biology, Chemistry, Physics, Algebra, Geometry, Trigonometry, Calculus, Economics, Statistics, US History, World History, Government and more." Files are stored and downloaded in Portable Document Format (PDF), a format used for all kinds of Internet downloads that can be read with Adobe Acrobat Reader, a program available free via the Web. Both Windows-based PCs and Macs can access these files. The mate-rials are competitively priced, easy to access, easy to download, and easy to pay for via credit card.

Free from the burden of a printed inventory and serving a tech-nologically sophisticated student audience, this company offers a model for creating electronic materials that may well compete suc-cessfully with their printed counterparts. PinkMonkey also benefits from the fact that the materials they are selling are relatively short, thus avoiding the present resistance to reading book-length mate-rials on-screen or having to print out a full-length book.

SELLING SUBSCRIPTIONS TO YOUR SITE

An option rapidly being adopted by reference publishers, the paid subscription site is probably familiar to most people in publishing through the online efforts of *Literary Market Place*. Scientific, med-ical, and technical publishers have also adapted this format, offering the convenience of accessing massive volumes of information and classic volumes from the home, office, or hospital.

Although such subscription sites have thus far only supplemented the printed versions on which they are based, it may well be that mas-sive printed volumes of time-sensitive and updated material will be the first to be replaced by electronic access. If, for instance, you rely on a publisher to offer updates, and those updates can be entered on a monthly, weekly, or daily basis online rather than annually or semi-annually in a print version, why wouldn't you prefer the online version? Not only does such a system save paper costs, but it adds service value for the consumer.

GIVING IT AWAY FREE

Often described as a gold mine of free information, the World Wide Web is now also the repository of a huge amount of book material, some of it offered by publishers themselves, some by public service sites, and some by other kinds of commercial sites. Certainly the most prominent provider of such materials is Project Gutenberg (*http://promo.net/pg*). Founded in 1971, with the intention of creating a public library of e-text versions of major works of literature in the public domain, the project has over 6,000 "e-texts" currently available. You can download classics such as *Anna Karenina* and *Moby Dick*.

Whereas Project Gutenberg is purely a public service, PinkMonkey offers free downloads of literary works as well, but it does so as a promotional service component of its commercial site. Currently, there are 1,800 works of public-domain literature available through PinkMonkey, including a selection of poems by Wordsworth, Henrik Ibsen's play *A Doll's House*, and Lewis Carroll's *Alice in Wonderland*. Whether the availability of these works online will affect sales differently than their free use through a public library remains to be seen.

While neither publishers nor authors are going to give away their copyrighted material over the Web if they think it will cost sales, posting excerpts and sample chapters is clearly a way to interest readers. Publishers are learning to post enough material on their own sites to engage a reader and convey the quality of the work. In addition, a few commercial sites post sample chapters of currently popular books; two worth looking at are BookBrowse (*www.bookbrowse.com*) and Dial-a-Book Chapter One (*www.dialabook.inter.net/Chapter One/index.html*). Each is interesting in its own way. BookBrowse, the more commercial of the two, offers publishers advertising opportunities, posts excerpts from bestsellers, and has its own newsletter.

While these sites are too new to determine whether or not they will have an impact on sales, they provide publishers with an excellent model of what can be done.

Marketing with an E-mail Newsletter

Truly a technological gift, it's hard to imagine a simpler or more cost-effective marketing vehicle than the e-mail newsletter. Through e-mail newsletters you can instantaneously deliver information and promotions, and because there aren't any printing or postage expenses, you can get your message out as often as you want. You can provide codes for tracking orders, and you don't even need a graphic artist to lay out your publication, just a database and someone to write the copy.

Depending on the kind of publishing you're doing, an e-mail newsletter can be used as a general marketing tool—to announce titles and promote brand identity—as a sales vehicle for generating orders, or both. You can create links to your Web site catalog for providing further information on specific titles, links to affiliated booksellers, or links to your own online order form.

Naturally, this has to be done with common sense and good taste. You can't bombard people with advertisements and expect them to respond enthusiastically, but if you can give them some legitimate, valuable information, they will look forward to receiving your e-mail newsletter and will surely buy more of your books.

Though, perhaps, out of proportion to the offense it causes, commercial e-mail or "spam" generates an immense backlash of ill will. It is, therefore, imperative that publishers adhere to Internet conventions and send newsletters only to those who qualify themselves as recipients, either by requesting information or at least passively indicating their willingness to receive some sort of news. You should also observe the convention of offering a click-through "unsubscribe" option with a polite announcement that those who have received your message in error or no longer wish to subscribe can easily opt out of future mailings.

You can begin to build this list through a number of methods. Offer visitors to your Web site the opportunity to subscribe. Provide information about your free e-mail newsletter in your books, catalogs, ads, and other promotional materials. Ask your authors for their contact lists. Finally, you can also ask subscribers to recommend friends and provide rewards when they do.

As with old-fashioned direct mail, your e-mail promotional efforts will be more effective if you contact people on a regular basis. But unlike direct mail, since you are downloading your message directly onto their computers, your selling needs to be a little more low-key. You should offer bargains, but you need to offer something else besides—something that people will be interested in reading for its own sake.

If you are maintaining some kind of news bulletin board on your Web site, you can make this part of your e-mail newsletter. If not, you might consider sending excerpts of forthcoming books, author interviews, and original articles.

Morgan Kaufman Pinpoints E-Mail Newsletters

A Harcourt imprint specializing in professional-level computer books and textbooks, Morgan Kaufman Publishers has chosen to focus its newsletter on telling readers about new titles. Each issue includes a promotion code—in essence an electronic coupon—that allows newsletter subscribers to purchase specified titles at a discount from the company's Web site.

Free from the need to achieve the high volumes dictated by print promotions, the company's e-mail newsletter can be customized to target even tiny segments within the publisher's mailing list. Not only does this mean that it can give readers a newsletter of greater interest, but it can attract subscribers more easily because they understand that they will get highly targeted material rather than a general company publication.

Morgan Kaufman offers subscribers thirteen subject categories—from high-performance computing to graphics programming to operating systems—within the company's larger list. Individuals can elect to receive the company's monthly newsletter and/or new book information in as many categories as they choose.

To build its mail list Morgan Kaufman offers a subscription option to Web site visitors and collects e-mail addresses at the many conferences and academic meetings where it exhibits. The company has found that post-conference e-mail book offers have been extremely successful because they can be narrowly targeted. As an example, the company featured the book, *Introduction to NURBS*, by Daniel F. Rogers, which deals with a mathematical method for describing graphic shapes, after a conference session on this topic. This book clearly has a limited, specialized audience, but being able to easily reach that audience is like having money in the bank for the publisher.

Specialized Booksites

Several Web sites provide marketing and publicity opportunities for publishers both commercially and as part of broader services. The following sites stand out at the moment as being particularly active, but before committing your resources, you should conduct your own investigation. A year in the Internet world can bring drastic changes and various new possibilities.

ReadersNdex

ReadersNdex (*www.ReadersNdex.com*) is a commercial site "partnering with publishers and booksellers." In practice, this means that they charge publishers for a "home site" and book listings. Book orders are automatically routed back to the Web site from which the user was referred—whether they came from a publisher's own site or bookstore. The default sales site, for readers who access ReadersNdex directly, or for publishers that don't sell direct, is the Tattered Cover bookstore in Denver.

Client publishers range from single-title presses to major corporate players. For the large publishers, the site simply amounts to an inexpensive ad and one more way to inform readers about their books. For the smallest publishers, the site may take the place of posting a Web site of their own. For midsize publishers, the site may be a simple way to promote their top titles and create further Web links.

BookZone

Closely affiliated with the Publishers Marketing Association and the Audio Publishers Association, BookZone (*www.BookZone.com*) offers many of the same services as ReadersNdex, creating publisher home sites with catalog descriptions of particular titles. Orders, whether through a link to the publisher or through BookZone's own ordering system, go directly to the publisher. BookZone also offers nonparticipating publishers a free link to their own site.

BOOKWIRE

A centralized site for the publishing industry, authors and publicists can take advantage of the Authors on the Highway section, which lists bookstore appearances by authors. Bookwire (*www.bookwire.com*) offers links to *Publishers Weekly, Library Journal,* and publishers' own Web sites. They also feature "The Book Report," a book review column originating with America Online, which features author interview/chat sessions as well as conventional reviews.

INTERNET PUBLICITY

In addition to the marketing and publicity opportunities offered by online booksellers, public relations opportunities—useful to both authors and publicists—are thinly scattered around the Internet. Since these seem to change almost daily, I will offer a simple overview of the kind of outlets available.

ONLINE REVIEWERS

While the number of serial publications—newspapers, magazines, newsletters—appearing online has mushroomed, most of these are simply online editions of their print versions, so that the review of your book that appeared in a particular newspaper or magazine may also show up on that publication's Web site.

There are, however, a few successful magazines that are published exclusively on the Web, as well as a few online editions of print publications that create separate content for their Web editions. The editors of these publications need to be treated in much the same way as your other media contacts. You can e-mail them a press release, but if they're interested in reviewing a book, unless you are already set up to download books on demand, you will ship them books just like the rest of your media contacts.

One place to look for further opportunities, however, is in creating links from a review to your own Web site. If the Web publication offers this option, then your solid online presence can pay off, especially for a niche publisher. The reader who is interested enough in a review of your fitness book to follow the link will then discover your entire line of fitness books and, in the best of all worlds, become a regular customer.

Authors Online

Authors who are active contributors to newsgroups or who already have their own Web sites are well positioned to promote their books through these outlets. If you're an author and not already involved, you can begin by researching and participating in newsgroups that deal with issues related to your book. These groups offer the opportunity to reach a large number of people who have demonstrated an interest in your topic through their own active involvement. You can reach them on a regular basis from your home, offer them your expertise, receive their feedback, and develop an understanding of people's interests and needs, which may be useful in future editions or new titles. Finally, you will also be making the acquaintance of many who are newly interested in your subject, just when they are most likely to be looking for information and buying a book.

There is, of course, an appropriate etiquette that restrains self-promotion among newsgroup participants, but you certainly can identify yourself as the author of such and such book. You can also refer people to a Web site, the author's or the publisher's, if substantive information is offered there in addition to promotional material about the book.

Authors and publishers should be aware of the opportunity to set up chat sessions with readers through online booksellers, and they should take advantage of the opportunity—offered by the major online bookstores—to enter comments in the bookseller's online listings. The more information available on a book in the online catalog, the more likely it is to be chosen by a reader browsing a particular subject.

8

Selling Beyond the Bookstore

A bookstore may seem like the easiest and most logical place to sell a book. Yet, because of the narrow margins, high rate of returns, and competition for shelf space, publishers in recent years have devoted substantial energy to cultivating supplemental and/or alternative markets. By doing so they have found new readers, increased their sales, and sometimes even improved their margins.

Following are descriptions and explanations of outlets and strategies for finding and cultivating some of these alternative markets. While most publishers adopt at least some of these strategies, my observation has been that, in general, alternative markets often represent strong growth potential, and for small publishers and niche publishers, making the most of alternative markets is absolutely critical.

NONBOOK RETAILERS

There is hardly a retail outlet you can walk into that doesn't carry at least a few books. Fabric stores, bike shops, park shops, sporting-goods stores, gift boutiques, kitchenware stores, health-food stores, stationery stores, art-supply stores, camera shops, religious shops, auto-supply stores, hardware stores, nurseries, toy stores, and pet shops: They all carry books, and the share of the market going to these retailers is growing.

If you publish books for railroad hobbyists, you are probably already selling through model shops, and if you publish sewing books, you undoubtedly sell to the independent and chain fabric stores. You may also work with the sales reps who visit these accounts as well as sewing-supply wholesalers and catalogers. For many niche publishers, nonbook wholesalers and retailers such as these represent a mainstay in their sales strategies. For others, such outlets may provide a nice incremental addition to their revenues. Publishers of regional books should also be familiar with the strategy of targeting a variety of local retailers as outlets, too. I have seen guides to local schools and guides for prospective homebuyers featured in grocery stores, pharmacies, convenience stores, and even a shoe repair shop.

One of the advantages of working with these stores is that most have never heard of the trade practice of returning unsold books. They are used to paying outright for the products they sell and often expect to pay immediately for products from small suppliers. On the downside, if books don't represent a significant part of their business, they're unlikely to put time or energy into selling them.

In addition, these retailers often don't have the space or appropriate shelving for displaying books. If you can help them by providing a point-of-purchase display or spinner racks, these can give you a nice edge in nonbookstore retail outlets. Long before most publishers recognized the importance of alternative retailers, Sunset Books placed spinner racks in hardware stores. At the time, there were very few other books to be found in the stores, if any, and so they had an exclusive, interested audience. These days I see books from lots of publishers in all kinds of stores with all kinds of point-of-purchase displays. In my local pharmacy I recently spotted a rather elegantly designed wood point-of-purchase display featuring die-cut, gift-style cookbooks. Such displays abound and are available in a wide range of prices.

Naturally, you need to manufacture the display cheaply enough and have a minimum order that is large enough so you can absorb the cost of the display and still make money on a single order. The real trick with a display of this kind, however, is to have some kind of sales follow-up—preferably in person by a sales rep or rack jobber, but if this isn't possible, then by phone—for taking orders to refill the display as it sells down. This turns your marketing effort from an incremental, frontlist sale to a backlist staple.

Heyday Books Targets Local Bicycle Shops

Early in my career, I did some work for Heyday Books, a small regional publisher with an emphasis on Native American studies, natural history, and outdoor recreation. With an experimental attitude in marketing and a clear vision of its audience, Heyday worked hard to reach a variety of nonbookstore retailers and found great success in park and museum shops and a variety of specialty stores. In fact, Heyday had a niche within a niche, publishing only in certain subject areas while maintaining a regional focus.

During the time I worked for Heyday, we published several local bicycling guides, which were targeted to a substantial audience of recreational cyclists. We were also quite sure that these books would be well suited for sale through bicycle shops. We found, indeed, that these shops did carry a few guidebooks as well as some bicycle repair manuals, but that the books were mostly consigned to an obscure shelf where they grew dusty and dog-eared—not an encouraging sight for the success we envisioned.

To encourage these retailers to stock the books and to optimize sales, in the true spirit of small-press publishing, the entire staff got together and hand-made a set of colorful cardboard point-of-purchase displays. We then threw the books and displays in our cars and set about calling on every small bike shop in a region encompassing several counties. We met the owners and managers, who were thrilled with the books when they saw them. We set up accounts on the spot, placed the displays on the sale

---

counter next to the cash register, and wonder of wonders, came back with a stack of checks from stores that were used to buying bicycle parts COD.

We followed up on these sales with phone calls at regular intervals over the next year or so and continued to receive substantial reorders. These efforts contributed to a profitable book and led to a profitable series.

TRACKING DOWN DISTRIBUTORS, WHOLESALERS, AND RETAILERS

In an ideal world, you would be familiar with the specialty retailers and wholesalers before you published a book in a particular field. In the real world, however, publishers often find themselves expanding in areas they had not anticipated, and so need to establish themselves in new and unfamiliar markets.

If this is your situation, I suggest you begin by visiting your local retailers in whatever specialty you are pursuing. Take a look to see if they carry books, and check to see if they stock a large selection from a broad range of publishers or just a few titles. Get to know a few managers or owners and ask them how they buy books, who they buy them from, and what kind of terms they are accustomed to. In addition, get the names of distributors and wholesalers. They can often give you contact names and phone numbers as well.

While you're visiting your local specialty retailers, you can also do a little market research by showing them your forthcoming titles and getting their responses. Draw them out about the positives and negatives. If you start early enough in the editorial process, you may be able to make use of their input on the content. These are the people you want to sell your book. They know what sells and what they want to sell. Now is the time for you to be a really good listener. One precaution to keep in mind: If you're publishing a cookbook that makes nasty comments about health-food stores, don't expect these retailers to sell your book. Naturally, the same is true for books that touch any specialty market, and while this should seem obvious, I've witnessed the embarrassment of publishers being turned down by offended buyers more often than I care to remember.

If you are developing a whole line of books for one of these specialty markets, you will probably want to invest some marketing dollars and efforts into becoming established in that industry. You'll probably want to attend the industry trade shows to meet important buyers, become familiar with the trade practices of the industry, and set up accounts with distributors, wholesalers, and retailers. This will also be a place to meet prospective authors (perhaps the featured speakers) and familiarize yourself with the current issues of importance in the industry. For locating information about trade shows, try the *Trade Show and Convention Guide*, published by Billboard Publications, Inc., or *Trade Shows Worldwide*, from Gale Research. One of these should be available in your public library.

A few inquiries are usually all that's required to bring you to the major players in any industry, but if you want to do any prior research or track down a wider range of potential wholesalers, take a look at *Wholesale and Retail Trade USA*, another comprehensive directory published by Gale Research.

If you have only one title that incidentally overlaps into a specialty market, you know it doesn't make financial sense to attend trade shows or even research the industry. It probably doesn't even make sense to try to set up a lot of accounts with businesses that, in any case, probably won't be interested in making special arrangements to buy just one book. In such instances, it might make more sense to contract with another publisher, one who specializes in this niche, either to distribute or license your overlapping title into a market that makes up a regular part of its business.

BUILDING A MARKET THROUGH ASSOCIATION SALES

A mainstay of scientific, technical, medical, and professional publishers, as well as academic presses, professional associations provide a lucrative, targeted audience for books that are closely affiliated with a particular subject matter. Association sales can add significantly to the bottom line for general trade publishers in a variety of niches, as well as publishers specializing in books that straddle the professional and trade marketplaces.

The first step in your association sales strategy is to locate the organizations and associations that would be interested in your line. If an area is new to you, the natural place to start is with your authors. To what organizations do they belong? Where do they speak? What professional meetings do they attend? If you have authors who are experts in their fields, they should be plugged into these associations already.

Their experience, however, may be narrow, and you are likely to find many more possibilities with a little research. Start with the *Encyclopedia of Associations,* published by Gale Research, a multi-volume set available in most large public libraries. Next, browse the Internet; many, if not most, professional organizations have Web sites. The information and links these sites provide will speed you along in your search.

Once you have identified the organizations and associations likely to be interested in your books, you need to locate the right person in the organization. This will usually be the director of marketing or the director of publications. Most professional associations will have one or more publications—catalogs, magazines, brochures, or newsletters—even if they don't publish books themselves, and these can be good avenues both for sales and reviews.

Due mostly to the cost, it's rare to have a membership organization use a book as a premium, but many associations sell books to their members through catalogs, onsite bookstores at conferences, and their own Web sites. Such sales make winners of the organization, its membership, and the publisher. Offering quality resources helps organizations fulfill their mission of serving their members and also provides a source of extra revenue. For association members, the convenience of one-stop shopping for professional materials is a valuable time-saver. For publishers, there is not only the benefit of incremental sales, but also the value of an implicit endorsement when a professional organization selects a book for inclusion.

BUYING ADVERTISING ON A PER-ORDER BASIS

Whether you are dealing with a large organization with its own slick magazine or a smaller association with a tiny newsletter, buying an occasional ad in its publication can be a nice way to show your support for the organization and garner some goodwill. If, however, you don't really have the money to invest in ads or you doubt whether you can come out ahead by buying these ads, another approach is to offer an exchange. Suggest that the organization run a coupon or direct-response ad with a toll-free number and that you will give it a certain percentage of each sale as a commission. The orders can come directly to you if the organization wishes, but you have to make sure you can track the source of your orders so that you really do pay the proper commission.

If the organization would rather take the orders itself, but doesn't want to inventory or ship the books, you can offer to drop-ship the order. Let the organization take the order and payment, then have it send you a mailing label, packing slip, and check, minus their commission. You cash the check and ship the books. It costs you nothing to make these sales, and the organization makes money as well.

THE VALUE OF ATTENDING CONFERENCES

While the core of your association sales strategy may be to locate organizations and set up accounts with them as resellers of your books, if your budget allows, you should make every effort to attend the conferences sponsored by these organizations. You can, of course, sell books at such events, but more important than sales, attending conferences gives you the opportunity to build relationships with association officials and members. You can promote your authors as speakers at these events, and you may well pick up new book projects. Finally, among the other exhibitors, you will often find associations and groups interested in offering your books through their own publications and events. In an era of increasing competition and decreasing margins, giving this kind of energy and attention to membership organizations and professional associations can well provide a solid foundation for the future of your company.

RECOGNIZING OPPORTUNITIES FOR PREMIUM SALES

Usually lumped under the rubric of special sales, books sold for premium use are often treated as simple bulk sales to nontrade institutions and offered at similar discounts. In fact, when the local chapter of a nonprofit organization purchases a book to give to new members, or a small company purchases copies to give to employees, their purchases—numbering perhaps in the hundreds—justify neither proactive marketing efforts nor a special discount schedule.

In contrast, sales to a large institution wanting to use a book to promote its product or services can number in the hundreds of thousands, easily justifying the time and expense of an aggressive marketing campaign. Such sales, though typically net priced—i.e., assigned a unit price with a fixed profit added to the manufacturing cost—can add significantly to a publisher's bottom line.

Unlike typical premium gifts—pen sets, frequent flyer miles, or cell phones—a book usually suggests itself for premium use when and because its subject matter relates directly to the object, product, subscription, or membership that it promotes. In many cases, this connection is an afterthought, an area to mine for extra sales, but for the publisher equipped to create a custom-packaged project, such sales can open up valuable opportunities for an expanded business focus.

Earthworks Press Customizes Books for Utility Companies

Earthworks Press, the publisher of the bestselling *50 Simple Things You Can Do to Save the Earth,* provides an immensely successful example of how to package a book for premium sales.

Having already sold a huge number of their lead title for premium use by companies that wanted to be identified as environmentally sensitive—mostly in response to inquiries from the companies themselves—Earthworks decided to develop spin-off titles for industries in particular need of educational and promotional materials.

At the top of Earthworks's target list were energy companies. Earthworks knew that these companies had been mandated by their governing utility commissions to allot money for conservation projects and were thus in need of appropriate materials. With this need in mind, Earthworks approached its regional energy supplier, Pacific Gas and Electric (PG&E), with two prospective titles: *30 Simple Energy Things You Can Do to Save*

---

the Earth and *25 Simple Things Kids Can Do to Save Energy.*
Earthworks offered PG&E the opportunity to customize the books
for its audience, developed a working relationship, and eventually
wrote an order for 500,000 books.

Building on this success, Earthworks's special marketing staff
then made cold calls to over one hundred energy suppliers and
simply asked for the person in charge of environmental affairs.
They used the book developed in conjunction with PG&E as an introduction and ultimately made sales to about twenty-five companies,
with orders ranging from 5,000 to 500,000 copies.

Each company received custom-produced books of sixty-four or
eighty pages and paid a flat price per copy depending on the quantity and how much the book was customized for its use. Since the
energy suppliers used the books as part of their educational
efforts—giving them away free to customers, at Earth Day fairs, in
school programs, and at appliance centers—none of the books carried a cover price, nor were they ever sold through retail outlets.

While Earthworks's spectacular success with custom-packaged
books cannot be duplicated easily, the use of books as premiums when
they support the purchase of a more expensive item is fairly common.
For example, Ten Speed Press has for a number of years annually sold
thirty thousand to forty thousand copies of *The Food Processor Cookbook* to the Conair Corporation, which in turn used the books as premiums to promote the purchase of their Cuisinart food processor. Ten
Speed sells the books on a negotiated net-price basis, and a positive
byproduct of these sales has been to keep alive a book whose trade
sales alone wouldn't justify reprinting.

As a sales category open to a wide range of nonfiction titles,
publishers can pursue the premium market systematically through
trade shows, publications, and sales representatives. Among the relevant trade journals are *Incentive* (355 Park Avenue South, New
York, NY 10010-1789; Tel. (212) 592-6456; *www.incentivemag.com*)
and *Potentials In Marketing* (Lakewood Publications, 50 S. Ninth
Street, Minneapolis, MN 55402; Tel. (800) 328-4329 or (612) 333-0471;

www.trainingsupersite.com). The Premium Incentive Show is produced by BillCom Exposition Conference (Dulles International Airport, P.O. Box 17413, Washington, DC 20041; Tel. (888) 202-1276).

MAIL-ORDER AND ONLINE CATALOGS

The largest catalogers and the largest segment in the mail-order catalog business belong by far to computer resellers. Other major mail-order categories include clothing, home furnishings, sporting-goods equipment, office supplies, and medical supplies. Yet despite the dominance of catalogs focused on high-ticket items directed to businesses and consumers, there are plenty of catalogs that sell books along with other products, and these offer ample opportunities to find additional avenues for your titles.

Mail-order catalogs featuring books cover a range of subjects and audiences. There are general consumer catalogs addressing different tastes, from the ubiquitous *Lillian Vernon* to Public Broadcasting's highbrow *Signals* and *Wireless* to the quirky *Things You Never Knew Existed*. There are hobbyist catalogs for gourmet cooks, sewers, craftspeople, and collectors, and, of course, specialized book catalogs serving specific religious interests or professionals.

Computer books and cookbooks are naturals for software catalogs and kitchenware catalogs respectively, and they have proven successful in this market. Hobby publishers especially may rely on catalog sales for a significant portion of their income. For most publishers, however, catalog sales will probably represent only a small slice of their revenue. Nevertheless, a little research into the market can produce valuable outlets for specialized topics.

Many mail-order catalogers are now adding Web sites, which for some consumers, is the first and favored point of contact. In addition, there are a number of catalog-oriented Web sites created by specialty retailers and associations, as well as online catalogs that have been established solely in this format. As noted previously, many online booksellers blend catalog and bookstore features—a trend that is already showing up in other kinds of online selling.

For information about the industry in general, take a look at the trade magazine *Catalog Age* (P.O. Box 4949, Stamford, CT 06907; Tel.

(800) 775-3777). Their Web site (*www.mediacentral.com*) contains a lot of valuable information and links to other resources on direct marketing. Two Web sites worth investigating are *www.cataloglink.com*, with a nice category index of traditional mail-order catalogs and *www.buyersindex.com*, with links to a huge number of online catalogs and sales opportunities. Also take a look at the *Shop at Home Catalog Directory*, a mail-order catalog that lists, describes, and offers over six hundred mail-order catalogs (7100 E. Bellview Avenue, Suite 305, Grenwood Village, CO 80311, Tel. (303) 843-0302). Two directories you may be able to find at the library are the *Catalog of Catalogs*, published by Woodbine House and the *Directory of Mail Order Catalogs*, from Grey House Publishing.

TAPPING THE MARKET FOR SUPPLEMENTAL TEXTS

Textbook publishing, as I noted in chapter 1, is a specialized field that rarely overlaps with trade and professional publishing. Text publishers market their books primarily through sales reps who visit schools and college campuses. These reps carry sample books and give away large numbers of review copies. They are familiar with current course offerings and the instructors, and part of their time is spent recruiting potential new authors among faculty. The textbooks they carry are written for a specific course or group of courses and contain all kinds of special features, such as chapter reviews and questions for study. As a consequence, these books are not usually of interest to readers outside the college market, and so the whole publishing concern operates within a closed world.

Because the text market is so tightly focused and specialized text publishers have such an established presence, it is by and large a tough and expensive market to enter. Nevertheless, college instructors do use and assign a lot of books in addition to the traditional texts, and opportunities abound for trade and professional publishers to sell books for supplementary reading on all subjects.

PLANNING AHEAD FOR CLASSROOM USE

If you foresee your books being used as supplemental texts, then you can directly strengthen their suitability for this market while they are still in the editorial planning stage. Ask yourself these three critical questions: Which specific course or courses might adopt this book as a supplemental text or resource? What exactly does your book bring to the student? What does your book do for the professor?

If your authors have academic connections, talk to them about the courses they teach as well as others that overlap into their field. If they indicate that there is a potential classroom use, you can make appropriate editorial changes. You can adjust the focus or tone of the presentation to appeal to college instructors, and you can make sure the information is formally substantiated through footnotes and bibliographies.

Promoting Course Adoptions through Direct Mail

I know a few niche publishers that personally make field sales calls to colleges within their region because supplemental text sales are a major portion of their revenues. Most trade and professional publishers, however, can't afford the time to visit colleges, nor would the investment make sense. For them, the primary means of encouraging textbook adoptions is through direct-mail marketing to college instructors.

Chapter 6 deals with basic principles of direct mail, and if you are considering mailing to professors, you should read that chapter carefully. I will restrict my comments here to the specifics of marketing supplementary texts.

Select an Appropriate List

Your first task in creating a supplementary-text marketing program is to decide for which course or courses your book would be suitable, and, as noted above, you should make full use of your authors' knowledge of the academic market.

If you have a specialty area that you contact repeatedly and regularly, you may be in a position to build your own list of instructors for these courses. Most publishers, however, depend on regularly updated, rented lists from companies such as CMG Information Services (P.O. Box 7000, Wilmington, MA 01887; Tel. (800) 677-7959; *www.cmgi.com*) or Market Data Retrieval (P.O. Box 2117, Shelton, CT 06484; Tel. (800) 333-8802; *www.schooldata.com*). If you are entirely new to this area, perusing these catalogs is a good way to get a sense of what this market looks like. You can find over four thousand college courses by title and see the number of instructors who teach each course, for both two-year and four-year colleges. Looking at these numbers will give you a sense of what kind of selectivity you can apply, whether there are more courses and instructors than you care to mail to, or whether you should create a simple package that won't be too costly in a small print run.

Craft an Attractive Offer

Because college instructors are used to receiving vast quantities of textbooks for free, either as examination copies or desk copies accompanying course orders, they tend to expect to get books for free. In fact, sending out free examination copies to college instructors is standard procedure for most publishers.

If, however, this policy would unduly stretch your budget, here are a couple of alternatives worth considering. Begin by informing the professor that you are a small publisher and can't afford to give away books. Explain that you will be glad to provide an examination copy for free on the condition that the book is adopted for a course by a certain date. If an order is not received by that date, either the book must be returned or the instructor will be billed. A second alternative is simply to say: We are a small, independent publisher and can't afford to give books away. We invite you to buy the book at a nice discount, plus we will refund you the cost or send another desk copy with your course adoption.

A third strategy is to offer a free examination copy while charging for shipping and handling. This policy not only reduces the publisher's marketing costs significantly, but hopefully encourages those instructors who are seriously interested in the book to respond while discouraging those who are always ready to take a book for free but aren't really open to adopting a new book. I know one publisher that averaged a 5 percent response rate to several such offers and subsequently wrote course orders for 15 to 18 percent of those who originally responded. The ultimate success of this program, however, is more attributable to the quality of the material, which was highly targeted to specific courses, than to the offer itself.

A fourth strategy is simply to offer the book for sale and include a small note indicating that examination copies are available to instructors of "appropriate courses." I know yet another low-budget publisher specializing in supplemental texts who does the majority of his promotions on 8½" × 11" one-fold self-mailers. On the outside he provides a photo of the book along with the indicia and address, and on the inside appears a brief description of the book, the table of contents, and a coupon offering a 20 percent professional discount. He does his mailings with commercial lists and reports a 2 to 5 percent response rate, in which actual paid orders outnumber requests for free examination copies by a margin of two or three to one.

While both of the publishers mentioned above are pleased with the results of their mailings, I would suggest to them, and to you, that one of the great advantages of direct-mail marketing is the ability to test offers. If you will be doing direct mail on a repeated basis, I would make such a test one of my highest priorities.

Write and Design an Effective Package

While all of the basic instructions in chapter 6 apply to packages promoting supplemental textbooks, here are a few specifics worth remembering.

Include, if you can, testimonial quotes from academics in the field you are targeting. If possible, you should have a quote that says what a great boon this book will be for the teaching of a particular class. Of course, you can say this in your text, but having the statement from a peer—preferably a well-known and respected peer—is that much more convincing.

Since the job of your direct-mail piece is to engage the enthusiasm of instructors, you should emphasize how this book will help them in their job as teachers. *That* is the benefit. If your book contains the information instructors are looking for, explains the concepts in an appealing way, and is clearly written, then your book will help students learn. This is good. But for instructors teaching courses, the benefit of using your book rather than another is that your book will facilitate their job, making them better teachers and their teaching easier. Your piece needs to address this concern.

In reading your letter or brochure, instructors should get a clear sense of the information to be found in your book, as well as the point of view and such special features as timelines, charts, bibliographies, or suggestions for future research. Be sure to include a table of contents—flushing out the titles if they are not adequately descriptive—as well as specifications for length, trim size, price, and so forth.

Provide a Simple Response Mechanism

Everyone is busy, college instructors included. Between the moment your target instructor conceives the desire to look at your book and the arrival of the book on his or her desk, you should make the process as easy and fast as possible. If you want a check, be sure to provide a simple response form and business reply envelope. If you don't need a check, give a phone number. If you are offering a free book, and you want to discourage frivolous responses, you can demand a formal request on departmental stationery.

Whatever you do, be sure to state your offer clearly. Contingencies—"If you do this, we will do that"—are problematic. Aim for a simple direct offer.

"Call today, and we will send you a free examination copy" is best.

"Send $4 for shipping and handling, and we will send a free examination copy" is good.

"If you want to consider the book for adoption, write to us on departmental letterhead, and we will send an examination copy with an invoice. If you decide to include the book on the syllabus for a class you are teaching, and we receive a course order within x days, we will cancel the invoice. Otherwise, you must either return the book or pay for it" is good for discouraging requests. I do, however, see such offers all the time.

If you expect the supplementary-text market to be important for your book, you need to create policies that encourage the interest of teachers.

PROMOTING COURSE ADOPTIONS THROUGH TELEMARKETING

Described by one practitioner as "a shallow draft boat good for niche markets as well as an excellent method for guerilla marketers," telemarketing offers the opportunity to speak to a large number of prospects on a personal level. You can use telemarketing to do market research and develop relationships, and you can look upon it as a way of hand-selling at a distance. You can use it to follow up on catalog or brochure mailings and to renew contacts made at conventions.

The medium works best, however, with pinpointed markets. Calling computer science instructors about a line of books on programming languages, for instance, is probably a strategy too diffuse to be effective. There are simply too many books and too many instructors. If, however, you are publishing books that would be useful in landscape architecture classes, you could conceivably call a large percentage, if not all, of the approximately six hundred instructors of these classes.

When developing an effective telemarketing program, the first principle to keep in mind is that experience helps. Whether you are doing the calling yourself, hiring or assigning employees to make the calls, or outsourcing the job to an agency, the people who make the calls will get better at communicating with your target audience as they continue with the process. They will learn the language of the instructors and identify recurring concerns, and they will learn what questions to ask and which points to emphasize. With this information, they can narrow the gap between themselves and the person at the other end of the line.

Also keep in mind that most calls will result in leaving messages, so you must be set up to take callbacks. If you have a different person receiving the inbound calls, that person must have the same training and experience as the person originating the call. At the same time, all your telephone reps should be trained in making follow-ups to instructors in each particular instructor's preferred style. If during the initial phone contact the instructor expresses an interest in seeing copies of your books, you should determine how the instructor would like to be contacted in the future—by letter, e-mail, or phone—and use that format.

Above all, whoever is working the telephone must be sensitive to the responses of the person on the phone. This should probably be underlined and in bold. A good telemarketer is good at listening. You can learn a tremendous amount about your potential market and what it wants by listening carefully, and this information can be invaluable to you as a publisher. Remember too, this whole process is about building relationships.

Finally, keep in mind that you can plant a suggestion that this or that book would be suitable for a particular class, and you can take an order, but you are not calling to make a sale. You are certainly not there to push a sale. While it may be possible to create a sale when you have a hesitant instructor, you can only do that once. An unhappy customer is not a repeat customer, and the entire value of marketing books as supplemental texts is in the repeat orders. Class orders of whatever size, when repeated semester after semester after semester, can be a wonderful support to your company.

Targeting the Elhi Market

While both the mechanics and politics involved in getting school textbook adoptions put the mainstream textbook market beyond the reach of all but a few large publishers, many small and medium companies flourish by providing support materials and curriculum aids to elementary and secondary school teachers. Though competitive, this piece of the "Elhi" market is accessible if you have quality materials. The fact is, teachers buy books, lots of them, and they are constantly on the lookout for anything that will help them in their work. Moreover, publishers whose primary goal is to sell to teachers are also profiting through incremental sales to bookstores, the homeschool market, and day-care facilities.

To reach teachers, you need to plug into specialized outlets that are for the most part separate but parallel to the consumer market. Brick-and-mortar teacher stores and education Web sites are frequented by teachers and parents alike. In addition, education magazines and professional journals provide a vehicle for promoting to teachers with different specialties and at different grade levels.

Publishers who are interested in exploring this market can begin by visiting *www.earlychildhood.com*, the Web retail arm of Discount School Supply, as well as their local teacher's store. The National School Supply and Equipment Association trade show is a key event in this market, paralleling the BEA for trade publishers, and offers an opportunity to see what's out there and make connections. There are, too, a number of specialty catalogs targeted to teachers in different disciplines and at different grade levels.

GEMS Cultivates Teachers One at a Time

When the Lawrence Hall of Science (LHS) was established twenty-five years ago in Berkeley, its palpable fingers-in-the-oobleck, hands-on approach broke new ground in science and math education. Working with kids directly in afterschool programs and daycamps, LHS staff invented activities designed to engage children's curiosity. They worked hard to make the process of experimentation and investigation playful for kids while teaching serious scientific concepts. They also taught local teachers how to adapt this approach to their classrooms.

The LHS publishing program, Great Expectations in Math and Science (GEMS) was an afterthought, a formalized presentation of the methods they had developed. In a sense, the books were conceived of as "anti-curricula curricula." They provide small discreet units of "replacement curricula," classroom activities that can involve anywhere from a single day to two weeks of class time. In fact, this flexibility is built into the books in response to the desire of classroom teachers.

With about seventy titles now in print, GEMS legitimately presents itself as a backlist publisher. And though six new titles are planned for each year, the major restriction in publishing more is the two-year development time required for each title. LHS staff chooses the most promising among the activities currently in development, writes them up, and takes them out to local schools for testing. On the basis of the results, the activities are rewritten and then tested nationwide. The book is rewritten yet again and finally published.

Despite the diligence and creative inventiveness of the LHS approach to science education, the market was at first slow to respond. Teachers were cautious about the new concepts, but the LHS name, which was established by this time, was reassuring.

Also helpful were the many good reviews in magazines and professional journals targeted to educators such as *Creative Classroom, Teaching Pre K–8* and *Teaching Children Mathematics*.

For GEMS, the central marketing challenge lies in the fact that their books are sold to teachers one at a time. Teachers buy the books with their own money to get ideas and techniques that will help them do a better job, and they're suspicious of anything that smacks of commercialism. Even so, GEMS direct marketing efforts have been effective. The publisher mails about 100,000 catalogs each year, and it sends out a newsletter twice a year that goes to somewhere between 40,000 and 50,000 teachers. These bring in a significant percentage of GEMS total sales.

The second major source of sales is from educational catalogs, including *Acorn Naturalists, Insect Lore, Delta Education, Constructive Playthings*, and the *National Science Teachers Association (NSTA) Catalog*. As the names imply, each has a specialty that overlaps with GEMS' core audience of science teachers and each adds a dimension to GEMS' marketing reach. Delta Education fields sales reps sell to school boards, NSTA sells at professional meetings, and Creative Playthings has it own retail outlets.

In recent years GEMS signed a trade distribution agreement with full-service distributor Consortium Book Sales & Distribution. Until that time they had a few active bookstore accounts and a steady stream of special orders, but they have never pursued the trade directly.

Those who are interested in developing the education market, whatever their specialty, should take note of GEMS' example. Building trust by creating consistently high-quality materials, GEMS communicates with teachers in their language, providing information and flexibility.

9

Subsidiary Rights

Loosely defined, subsidiary rights pertain to all the ways the contents of a book can be used other than in its original form—magazine articles, films, translations, calendars, audio versions, CD-ROMs, and so forth. On a shrinking planet with a seemingly insatiable hunger for information and entertainment that is served by an increasingly competitive and ever-broadening range of media, it's no wonder these rights should increase in importance to all concerned. Having a focused strategy and efficient procedures for handling these rights is imperative both for publishers and authors.

SERIAL RIGHTS

Generally more important for promotional purposes than as a source of supplementary income, the term "serial rights" refers to the use of excerpts in magazines and newspapers. These can be as extensive as the reprint of several chapters within several issues of a periodical, or as limited as the reproduction of a single photograph, drawing, table, or chart. As a publisher you should have a strategy for promoting your books through these rights, and as an author you can use them to build awareness of your work, widen your audience, and build your career.

FIRST SERIAL RIGHTS

Called "first rights" because they grant serial publication prior to book publication, the financial allocation and handling of these rights is often open to negotiation between authors and publishers. While publishing contracts usually specify a fifty-fifty split between authors and publishers for most subsidiary rights, writers who are active in selling their work to magazines or newspapers can negotiate to retain these rights for themselves. On the other hand, those whose writing careers are secondary to other lines of work, or who have trouble marketing their own work, may well be glad to have their book publisher marketing these rights for them.

Aside from locating and contacting the appropriate markets for these sales, the biggest difficulty in selling first serial rights is the lead-time involved. Monthly magazines may need to see manuscripts six months or more in advance in order to schedule a piece, and publishers rarely have a polished manuscript early enough to make these contacts. In contrast, writers who specialize in a particular subject matter and consistently write for particular kinds of publications may be able to polish a chapter or chapters to submit to magazines well before a complete manuscript is delivered to the publisher. In this way the writers make the extra sale and also alert magazine editors to the fact that they have forthcoming books, a fact that hopefully increases their value in the editors' eyes.

A further consideration for authors and publishers is the amount of money involved in the sale of these rights. While the sale of first serial rights for a celebrity biography, a new novel by a blockbuster author, or a movie tie-in makes the news once or twice a year because of the dollar amount involved, such sales obviously represent an extreme. Most first-serial-right sales based on forthcoming books simply get paid at the same rate as any other original article. Authors and publishers who are engaged in selling these rights on a regular basis will have a sense of what represents a reasonable payment. Those who are new to the sale of these rights or who are selling to a new market would do well to consult the most recent issue of *Writer's Market* (Writer's Digest Books) to get a sense of how much magazines are paying. While not comprehensive in its coverage of potential outlets, this book can also be used as a tool for locating appropriate outlets for articles.

One issue that authors and publishers new to the area of serial rights need to be aware of is the issue of exclusivity. When selling first serial rights, you are usually giving a publication exclusive use of particular material prior to book publication. You can, of course, sell different chapters or portions of chapters separately, each as an exclusive, but the principle of exclusivity applies to each selection. In addition, national publications usually specify that they are buying "North American rights."

SECOND SERIAL RIGHTS

Usually considered a publicity function by publishers, second serial rights refer to the sale of excerpts after book publication. In general, magazines and newspapers pay very small amounts for these rights, but the promotional value can be great, and your audience for these rights can be broad. You should look upon every publication with an overlapping audience as a possible outlet. Selections from a travel book, for instance, might appeal to family publications, magazines targeted to seniors, outdoors or sports magazines, and regional publications, as well as mainstream travel magazines and newspaper travel pages. Authors who are looking for new markets can use these submissions as a way to make contacts in new subject areas by offering to customize articles for particular publications.

Newspapers and regional publications, by the way, are usually concerned with exclusivity only within their circulation areas, so that in working with them you can usually simply offer the material for "one-time use" or "simultaneous rights," meaning that the piece is sold with only geographical limitations on later sales.

Because your primary motivation in selling second serial rights is promotional, you should time your efforts to have reprints appear as soon after book publication as possible. You should also try to get a thorough and prominent credit line for the book. You can usually push to have publisher information appear, and many publications are willing to include a toll-free number. So, if part of your marketing strategy is to build your direct sales, make the inclusion of your toll-free number a negotiating point when selling reprint rights.

PAPERBACK RIGHTS

If the sale of paperback rights, whether mass market or trade, is a regular feature of your publishing program, then it's important for you to develop relationships with the editors at paperback houses who cover the hardcover publishers in your field. You should take the time to visit these editors, send catalogs highlighting your most important titles, and maintain regular correspondence, keeping them up to date on what rights are available. You need to establish a presence in the market so that you can get adequate attention for your titles, and you need the knowledge to negotiate favorable deals. You also need to know how to conduct auctions when the opportunities arise.

Even if you only sell paperback rights occasionally, it's important to understand when it's in your best interest to sell the paperback rights and how best to go about such a sale. Presumably you're considering selling paperback rights to another house because it promises, through its size and marketing clout, to sell many more copies than you could and to sell them much faster. Nevertheless, whether you decide to publish the book yourself or sell the rights depends on several factors, and there isn't always one simple answer.

An important primary consideration, of course, is finances. Will you come out ahead by selling the book? Most publishers making this decision try to project two years' sales of their own trade paper edition and their profit on those sales. If, for instance, you project a $20,000 profit, then—given a fifty-fifty split of subrights with the author—you will be looking for something like a $40,000 royalty advance from the paperback publisher. Naturally, the value of having the money sooner rather than later will affect your decision, as will your degree of confidence in your projections.

Equally important to the financial question is how important the book will be for the marketing of your entire line. If you have a big book that will pull your other titles behind it and help establish the identity of your company, keeping the rights and publishing the trade paper edition may be more important than the cash infusion. On the other hand, if you see the book as important over the long term but need the cash now, you may want to go ahead with the sale of rights. You can always take back the rights and reintegrate the book in your line when the contract expires in five or seven years. In the meantime, you can continue to sell the hardcover, however few the numbers, for the sake of maintaining the book as part of your company's identity.

Ideally, you will make the decision on whether to sell or retain rights during the preparation of the hardcover, so you can conclude the sale about the time your publicity hits and reviews begin to appear. These will naturally spur interest, and if strongly positive, increase the amount you can get.

Once you have decided you want to sell rights, your first step is to send out materials to the appropriate editors. In addition to sending the book, either as a manuscript or as proofs, you should provide any information that will help establish the author's credibility—other publications, sales history of previous books, professional expertise, and experience in promoting his or her work. Publishers will also probably want to know about your print run and/or the number of copies you have sold, depending on where you are in the book's publication cycle.

If you think you will have multiple offers, you will probably want to conduct an auction. You should make sure to have materials in publishers' hands at least three to five weeks prior to the auction.

GUIDELINES AND RULES FOR A PAPERBACK RIGHTS AUCTION

If you opt for an auction, the first thing to decide is whether or not to set an in-house floor—a minimum at which bidding must start. If you have no intention of publishing a paperback edition, would any amount be welcome? If not, what is the minimum you will really take? If only one publisher submits a bid, will you be satisfied with the minimum you set? Are you prepared to push for more with the knowledge that you might scare away all your potential buyers? Put some thought and hard-nosed analysis into this, so you can be as clear as possible about what a book is worth to you and what you want before you begin.

At this point, you should also decide whether or not you are willing to allow an interested publisher to set an outside floor. In this scenario, the publisher guarantees you a certain amount, and at the same time reserves the option to purchase rights by bidding 10 percent over the top competing bid. Publishers will use this strategy to scare away competition, and in some cases this can cost you. On the other hand, you will open the auction knowing you have a substantial minimum that you are guaranteed—presumably well above the inside floor you might have set—even if no one else is prepared to compete for the book.

Having established your policy regarding a floor, you will now send out letters to interested editors announcing the date and rules of the auction. Be sure to specify the exact rights available, the territory, and the terms. Set the date and time by which first bids must be submitted (being sure to specify the time zone), and enumerate the rules regarding incremental increases on subsequent rounds. All of this information should be included in a closing letter that potential buyers should receive about one week prior to auction. Here is a model closing letter.

Dear [Name],

I'm pleased that you and your colleagues are enthusiastic about [book title] by [author's name]. We just received a wonderful review in [name], which I am faxing along with this letter.

I've set the closing for [date]. I'd like to receive first bids by fax no later than [time and time zone]—any time before that is fine. These first-round bids will be confidential.

At [time], I will begin the second round with the lowest bidder and proceed upwards to the highest bidder, continuing in rounds until the conclusion of the auction. Offers must be increased in at least [x] percent increments.

Territory: North American reprint rights

Term: seven years

Please specify trade or mass market, advance, payout, and royalties. We are very interested in your marketing and promotion ideas as well.

*If you need any further information before [date], please let me
know. I look forward to hearing from you.*

Sincerely,

[Your Name]

On the day of the auction you will begin by phoning the lowest bidder
and inviting an offer to top the highest bid. You will then proceed
through the round and subsequent rounds until a winner is deter-
mined. Note that the letter above asks for marketing and promotion
ideas. If you will weigh a strong commitment to marketing against a
higher bid, you should make this known.

FOREIGN RIGHTS

While it's becoming more common for agents to sell North American
or English-language rights for their big books—holding back translation rights to sell separately—most U.S. publishing contracts grant
world rights to the U.S. publisher. This means that the American
publisher has the right and responsibility for selling foreign and translation rights wherever a deal can be made. As with other subsidiary
rights, advances and royalties earned from these sales are customarily
split between the publisher and the author.

Depending on the number of titles and profitability of foreign-
rights sales to their companies, publishers vary in how they conduct
their foreign-rights business. Some work with agents exclusively.
Others handle the bulk of foreign-rights sales in-house, relying merely
on agents for a few difficult markets—particularly Japan, Korea, and
Taiwan—where it's extremely important to have someone on the
ground, familiar with the players and up to the minute on changing
conditions. Interestingly, even larger publishers that typically handle
all their foreign rights find that it pays to hire an agent to represent
their big books for different languages and markets.

Following a format similar to the standard publishing contract,
translation rights typically involve an advance, usually equivalent to
the royalties projected for the first printing, and an escalating royalty

schedule. At present royalties for Asia begin at 6 percent. Latin America starts at 8 percent, and Europe varies from 7 to 9 percent. Both advances and royalties are, of course, negotiable, especially when dealing with a big book.

Those who plan on taking an active part in their foreign rights sales should plan on attending both the Frankfurt Book Fair (held each October) and BookExpo America (held each May or June) in order to meet as many foreign publishers as possible. Over the years, you will naturally be doing business with a fixed group of publishers on a regular basis. Presenting your lists to them directly and personally is vital.

If you want to expand your list, you could go through the *International Literary Market Place* prior to these shows, write to new prospects, and set up appointments. It should be noted that the standard procedure for publishers at these shows is to set up half-hour appointments back to back, so you need to go prepared with tip sheets, sales information, reviews, and a polished presentation.

Those who make foreign rights a year-round, full- or part-time job can also target new-to-them, foreign-language publishers by carefully reading the articles on international markets that appear regularly in *Publishers Weekly*. Offering good overviews on a market-by-market basis, the articles usually describe the major players in each and the books they publish. In addition, the advertising section accompanying these articles can prove useful in identifying good prospects.

BOOK CLUBS

Because they pay so little for the books they adopt, and because their marketing seems to be so powerful—especially to target audiences—small publishers sometimes feel that they will actually lose income by selling to clubs. In fact, all the evidence I have seen (and this evidence is purely subjective), has indicated that book clubs not only provide incremental sales but also help publishers in their marketing efforts.

I therefore recommend that publishers pursue book clubs whenever possible. As with paperback rights, your effectiveness in this area will improve as you develop relationships with the club editors. To begin, you should consult the latest *Literary Market Place* for a complete list of all clubs and editors. I emphasize the latest, because over the last few years ownership of the largest clubs has changed, with Bertelsmann having consolidated ownership of all the former Doubleday clubs and Book-of-the-Month club offerings under the Bookspan name. You can find information about the Bookspan group of clubs at *www.bookspan.com* and *www.booksonline.com*. Under the pressure of competition from Internet booksellers, Bookspan continues to experiment with new clubs and discontinue others.

A few of the largest clubs—Book-of-the-Month Club, Quality Paperback, Literary Guild—offer a wide variety of titles to the general consumer. Most, however, are specialized—there's a book club for people interested in crafts, a military book club, and several business-oriented book clubs, just for starters—so if you are a niche publisher serving the same audience as a particular club, you will certainly profit from developing a long-term relationship with that club. Not only will you sell to the club book after book, but your presence in its catalog will help promote awareness of your line to a group of readers dedicated to your subject area.

For maximizing the chances of having a book adopted, you should start early. Sending a manuscript or galleys four months before publication is minimum. Six months or more is better. When buying for a main selection, the larger clubs will often print their own editions or join in on your printing. This is where the longer lead times become critical. Smaller clubs, buying specialty titles in small quantities, will buy the books directly from you.

As a footnote here, specialty clubs will occasionally buy titles already in print, even backlist titles, if they are appropriate for their audience and if they think their buyers are unfamiliar with the book. I actually sold a ten-year-old professional volume to a club, much to the satisfaction of all parties involved. The numbers involved were small, but the club eventually reordered and sent the book into a new printing.

When negotiating with book clubs, you should be aware that, as standard procedure, they follow a pricing formula and offer two kinds of arrangements: "royalty inclusive" and "royalty exclusive." Royalty inclusive means the club pays you, the publisher, a set price per volume. It is then up to you to determine what portion of that price applies to your manufacturing costs and what portion represents the royalty or licensing fee—in other words, the portion that ordinarily would be divided between the publisher and the author. A royalty exclusive arrangement means the club pays a fixed amount for the manufactured book, or rather, it manufactures the book and then pays the royalty or licensing fee as a separate amount.

In either case, the book club will be limited in the amount they can spend—typically somewhere around 25 percent of the price they charge for the book. Since part of the club's marketing strategy is to discount books from the cover price, the publisher's share does not amount to much. Still, my basic approach is to get as much as I can, take advantage of the promotional value of having a book club selection, and appreciate the incremental income.

I should add here that when editors very much want exclusive rights to a book for which there is competition, they can occasionally go beyond the standard formula. In addition, when two clubs are competing for exclusive rights to a book, you can conduct an auction similar to the paperback auction described previously. You also have the opportunity to bargain when a club wants to reorder. You are not required to sell them more at the same price as the first sale, and because they are in the position of trying to fill orders from customers, you do have some leverage.

AUDIO RIGHTS

According to the Audio Publishers Association (APA), spoken-word audio products now account for approximately $1.6 billion and over sixty million units sold annually. With occasional exceptions, these audios are adapted from books by print publishers, or by audio-only publishers that buy rights from book publishers. They are sold in bookstores, by the large discounters, and by specialty retailers, including New Age and metaphysical stores, body-and-bath stores, health-food stores, audio-only stores, video stores, and truck stops. They are also sold through mail-order catalogs, at conferences, and through religious institutions.

The subject matter of these audios is as diverse as the outlets would indicate, and they attract an audience interested in a wide range of subjects, including fiction in all genres—literary, children's, romance, mystery, and horror—as well as most major nonfiction categories—religious and inspirational, business and motivational, self-help, biography, history, instructional, and foreign language. Given the size and the breadth of the market, spoken-word audio—either as a supplementary line or through sub-rights—can play a role in contributing to the profitability of many, if not most, publishers.

Whether you decide to develop audio in-house or look to sell audio rights to a company already established in the audio market will depend on a variety of factors, including whether you want to expand into something that in many ways amounts to an entirely new business. If you want to develop your own audio line, you will need to learn about, or hire people who know something about, audio production techniques. You'll be dealing with a different kind of packaging. Your sales reps will often be selling to a different set of buyers, and your accounting systems may need to be customized for special circumstances that apply in audio publishing.

SIZE MATTERS

As with any form of publishing, economies of scale apply. So for most publishers, the determining factor whether to publish audio or sell the rights will be the size of their line. Is it large enough to justify the investment of time and capital to develop expertise in this area? That said, I have encountered numerous small publishers, authors, and self-publishers who have experimented successfully with audio publishing.

These people tend to work with packagers who provide a range of technical services, including professional readers, recording, editing, duplication, and assembly of the finished product. (A list of packagers, as well as a host of valuable material on audio publishing in general, is available on the APA Web site at *www.audiopub.org*. You can write them at 627 Aviation Way, Manhattan Beach, CA 90266, or phone (310) 372-0546.) This leaves publishers and authors free to concentrate on the editorial side, with which they are usually most at home, and the marketing, which requires their own efforts.

Those who are most successful with this kind of arrangement serve a narrowly defined and highly targeted market—authors who supplement their incomes by selling tapes at workshops and seminars, or publishers that target what often amounts to a sectarian market. However, for those who envision a wider audience but have a small number of books suitable for audio, selling the audio rights to an established audio publisher can make a lot of sense. Grady Hesters, past president of the Audio Publishers Association and CEO of Audio Partners, Inc. (an audio publisher and direct-mail cataloger), suggests that "to have an adequate presence in the market, a publisher needs to have about twenty active titles and three to five new titles per season, and these numbers are minimums. Publishers that don't foresee developing an audio program at this level should probably sell subrights to an audio publisher."

Those who can make this minimum and want to maintain control of their audio versions will appreciate the following example.

New World Library Publishes Print and Audio

New World Library offers a model that many small and midsize publishers would be happy to emulate. With a strong line of self-help, inspirational, and New Age titles, the company's audio line contributes 15 to 20 percent of the total sales. Over the years, it has had two titles that have sold over a quarter of a million copies in audio: Shakti Gawain's *Creative Visualization,* with steady sales over almost twenty years, and Deepak Chopra's *The Seven Spiritual Laws of Success,* which sold as many in less than three years.

With rare exception, the audio line is adapted from books that the company has originated. All the presenting is done by authors, and while New World Library outsources the recording, the editing is done in-house. A major key to the company's success with audio has been its ability to promote a book and its audio version together. Finding it difficult to promote a stand-alone audio cost-effectively, the company includes both print and audio versions in every advertisement, listing, and press release. Naturally, author appearances help in the sales of both formats.

For both print and audio distribution, New World Library works with Publishers Group West, and even though retailer orders go through wholesalers, the company actively supports these sales through active marketing efforts. It mails almost four thousand catalogs to bookstores, New Thought churches, and specialty shops. And it identifies a core list of about seven hundred stores that do a large majority of the business. In addition to retail sales, New World Library actively pursues other markets for its audio line. It licenses audio rights to audio clubs such as Columbia House, Audio Book Club, and Doubleday Direct, and it sells to direct-mail catalogs such as Audio Editions and Audio Adventures.

New World Library's success in the audio field reflects consistently high-quality editorial content in a subject area that has been popular since the inception of spoken-word audio and steady efforts at marketing. Above all, they have built up a niche identity that serves them well in either format. Publishers considering their own line of audio must attend to these factors.

AUDIO FORMATS AND SPECIALIZED MARKETS

Spoken-word audio is currently sold in three formats: abridged cassette, unabridged cassette, and CD. The vast majority of these are naturally abridged, and the primary reason is cost. To put an entire book on cassette typically requires four to ten cassettes and sometimes more. These make expensive purchases.

There are, however, plenty of unabridged cassettes available directed to an enthusiastic listening audience. The sixty-four–page *Audio Editions* consumer catalog—with spoken-word audio from over one hundred publishers—offers about 40 percent of its titles in unabridged formats as well as a handful of CDs. Mailing over 2.5 million copies a year, the catalog offers a variety of titles ranging from language instruction to popular genre fiction by such authors as Mary Higgins Clark, Danielle Steel, and Louis L'Amour, to self-help and inspirational favorites such as *Don't Sweat the Small Stuff* and *The Celestine Vision*, to National Public Radio mainstay Garrison Keillor.

In contrast to the mass-market appeal and high-volume approach of *Audio Editions* is the specialized approach of Blackstone Audiobooks. Boasting a catalog with over 1,300 unabridged titles, including such seemingly obscure items as a sixteen-cassette edition of *The Education of Henry Adams*, Blackstone focuses on the rental market. With a direct consumer base of over thirty thousand customers, it has built a business to serve a particular audience and answered the problem of size and volume in an imaginative manner.

What about the large publishers you might expect to define the business? Simon and Schuster Audio (S&S) features both fiction and nonfiction in abridged and unabridged versions and even does a few titles on CD. For S&S, however, volume is the key to success. It boasts the all-time audio bestseller *Seven Habits of Highly Effective People*, by Steven Covey, with sales surpassing 2 million copies, and they offer such popular works as *Angela's Ashes*, by Frank McCourt, in abridged, unabridged, and CD formats. As noted, the use of CD is rare for spoken audio—probably because of the disadvantage of not being able to restart a CD at the point it was turned off—but S&S has pursued the unusual venture of a fully dramatized series of science-fiction classics, Alien Voices, directed by *Star Trek*'s Leonard Nimoy, and such a specialized recording may point a future direction for the format.

MARGINS AND MANUFACTURING

When deciding whether to sell audio subrights or create an audio line, there are some basic manufacturing and inventory issues to consider. Appalling as it sounds, margins for audio can be even smaller than for printed books, with the typical manufacturing cost for a cassette and its packaging running higher as a percent of retail than the print version.

On the positive side, because cassette duplication doesn't require the same elaborate setup as printing, smaller numbers can be produced without driving up costs and with a very quick turnaround. Audio publishers will often print the packaging that surrounds cassettes in what would amount to a relatively economic print run and then store a large percentage of these flat, duplicating cassettes and assembling the packages as needed.

AUTHORS VERSUS ACTORS

Look over a shelf of spoken-word audio and you'll find a mix of professional readers and authors. While no rule applies completely, it generally seems that print publishers experimenting with audio—seeing the audio version as a simple add-on—tend to have the authors present their own works. In contrast, for audio-only publishers, each audio represents their line, and the quality of the performance is a critical factor for long-term and short-term success.

Audio Partners, for instance, boasts a series of eminent classic and contemporary works presented by well-known actors and actresses, including Julie Harris (presenting *The Diary of Anne Frank*), Ed Asner (reading John Hersey's *Hiroshima*), and Robert Redford (narrating the documentary *The Language and Music of the Wolves*). A highlight in Audio Partners's catalog is a series of British imports featuring, among others, unabridged classics of works by Thomas Hardy, Jane Austen, and Charles Dickens that are read by world-renowned actors and actresses. For such works, the use of distinguished presenters clearly enhances the value of the package.

IF YOU WANT TO SELL AUDIO RIGHTS

If you decide to sell the audio rights to your books, here are some of the questions you should consider and points you will want to negotiate.

Large House or Niche Publisher?

As with print publishers, the range of audio publishers includes giant players, such as Time Warner and BDD Audio, and a number of midrange companies, such as Brilliance, Audio Renaissance, and Publishing Mills. There are also numerous smaller companies with specialized lines.

As one of the big kids on the block in this market, S&S buys audio rights from other publishers in addition to publishing the audio editions of its own books. And while the S&S list tends to split about evenly between fiction and nonfiction, that balance is not a stated goal. Rather, S&S looks for "strong titles in any category." The line is sold by the S&S Pocket Book sales force, which reaches a wide range of outlets from bookstores to truck stops.

Having the strength of this sales force behind your audio edition is clearly an advantage. If, however, your title appeals to a particular niche and is likely to get lost in a large line, you might be better off with a smaller publisher that can offer greater flexibility. The *APA Resource Directory* is a good place to start if you want to locate a broad range of companies.

Royalties and Advances

Like print publishing contracts, audio contracts have clauses both for advance size and royalty schedules. Industry standards put royalties at around 10 percent of net sales with stepped arrangements at different levels of sales. While this number does represent an average, royalties can range anywhere from 7 to 15 percent.

In addition, advances, except for very popular titles and authors, are typically low and range from $1,000 to $5,000. As a rule of thumb, audio publishers project their unit sales at about 10 percent of print sales and calculate an advance equivalent to the royalty of their own first printing.

Marketing Opportunities

Because the net income from an audio version of any one book may be disappointingly small, print publishers often neglect the audio market. Nevertheless, working with an audio publisher can provide the opportunity to expand the market for a title, since bringing out an audio version provides additional promotional opportunities and publicity.

Authors are usually very pleased to see their works in audio and, if they are skilled presenters, can often be called upon to do the reading. Even so, audio publishers will want the option of choosing a professional reader.

In either case, the audio format usually reaches people who complain they don't have enough time to read, so by offering the audio version both authors and publishers benefit by reaching an enlarged audience.

FILM AND DRAMATIC RIGHTS

Often regarded as the pot of gold at the end of the rainbow—especially for fiction publishers—rights for movies or television adaptations are usually handled by specialized agents. Nevertheless, publishers approached about selling these rights should at least understand how these deals are structured.

Dramatic rights are usually first negotiated as contracts with "options." A somewhat foreign concept to most publishers and authors, the option arrangement most resembles a lease with an option to buy. Producers pay the holder of the rights, usually author and publisher, for reserving the right to buy during the time it takes for them to put together a deal to produce a film, television program, or other dramatic presentation. If they do put together the deal, they exercise the purchase clause of the contract. If they fail to put together a deal, they let the option expire, but the original option fee remains the property of the author and publisher.

Among the terms usually negotiated in a dramatic rights contract are the option price and sale price, the length of time for which the option is held, terms for renewal of the option, whether the buyer has the right to publish the screenplay, and rights for sequels. Authors should be aware that they will have little or no say in how their work is treated.

Prices for dramatic rights—whether film, television, or any other kind of performance—naturally vary with the popularity of the original work, but as a basic rule, the price of the option is applied to the sale price if the option is exercised and the work is produced. Occasionally, producers who are enthusiastic about a work but have failed to put together a production deal will want to renew their option. This circumstance can be negotiated separately, but usually the price for renewal is not applied to the sale price. Occasionally, options for a particular work will sell repeatedly without a production ever being consummated. I've heard and read of Hollywood screenwriters who have made good incomes selling options for works that are never produced.

ELECTRONIC RIGHTS

Although currently an area undefined and still in its infancy, publishers, authors, and agents are all jealously guarding these electronic rights, awaiting the windfall that they hope will come from an unnamed source. In the meantime, here is a brief description of the various electronic formats in use or under development and how they are being treated.

Publishers should note that when negotiating author contracts, they need to look carefully at the issue of rights for media not yet created.

Some excellent sources of information on this and related legal questions include *The Copyright Guide* by Lee Wilson (Allworth Press), two books by Jonathan Kirsch, *Kirsch's Guide to the Book Contract* and *Kirsch's Handbook of Publishing Law* (both from Acrobat Books), and a number of online articles at "The Publishing Law Center" (*www.publaw.com*).

Aggregators

Described as service agencies that provide downloadable materials from many sources, some aggregators specialize in specific kinds of information—journal articles from academic presses, for instance, or scientific literature, or medical information—while others provide broad access to consumer magazines, newspaper articles, and a host of other sources. Lexis-Nexis, a division of publishing giant Reed Elsevier, is a prime example of the online information service provider. It offers academic, legal, governmental, and business information from a variety of sources, both among its own subsidiaries and from other publishers. Service agencies pay royalties to publishers for materials they sell as downloads.

Electronic Books

About the time the first edition of this book was going to the printer, e-books loomed on the horizon as a revolutionary format that could change the way publishers do business. Articles on new products and predictions about the inevitability of e-book dominance seemed to be appearing almost daily. Even so, questions remained about the technology, and whether readers would choose an e-book format over its conventional printed counterpart.

Five years later, the hype has diminished and publishers are still waiting for the answer to these questions. The dedicated e-book readers, so much in the news for a couple of years, have failed to establish themselves in the marketplace. RocketeBook and SoftBook both became Gemstar products, but there is no indication that they will survive. The Peanut Reader is now part of the Palm product line, which means there could be a large potential base of readers, but it is unclear whether more than a very few people have an interest in reading a book in this format.

The true players in this marketplace, whatever the size, for the moment are the Microsoft Reader and the Adobe Acrobat eBook (based on the earlier GlassBook technology). Available for use on Windows and Mac computers, they basically offer readers a chance to carry books on their laptops or read on their desktops. As with the dedicated e-book readers, however, publishers are still watching to see if there is a real market for these formats, and none of the companies actively involved are willing to release sales information.

As of this writing, my advice to independent publishers remains the same. The wisest course is to watch and wait, but secure e-book rights when signing new contracts.

CD-ROMs AND SOFTWARE

At one time both hailed and feared as the format that would finally kill the printed book, CD-ROMs have become the medium of choice for database and directory publishers. Its impact on the rest of the industry, however, has been small.

Because a single disk can replace such a huge amount of paper, and at the same time offer the ability to search and download, it is perfectly suited to replace massive amounts of information and multivolume sets. Some reference publishers have taken advantage of the format and done especially well, at the same time keeping up with the changing habits and expectations of consumers. The CD-ROM format has not, however, essentially altered the publishing or marketing process for those who develop such materials. They are simply selling disks rather than volumes, and in most cases they are selling both.

In contrast, the impact of CD-ROMs on the encyclopedia market does offer a lesson for publishers that choose to ignore new technologies. The advent of the home computer and CD-ROM encyclopedia has proven catastrophic to those companies slow to adapt. In this case, the expense of a set of encyclopedias, long seen by parents as an investment in their child's education, has been replaced by the purchase of a computer, which now comes bundled with a CD-ROM encyclopedia.

Elsewhere, the impact of software and CD-ROMs on the traditional book has been rather spotty. While many computer-book publishers offer book-disk combinations, the disks supplement the books rather than vice versa. There are some electronic versions of cookbooks, instructional products, and even crossword puzzles, and there are various software adaptations of children's favorites.

LICENSING

According to Nolo Press's online legal dictionary, licensing involves "giving written permission to use an invention, creative work or trademark. A license provides a way to make money from your invention or creative work without having to manufacture and sell copies yourself." Under this broad definition, all the subsidiary rights considered in this chapter might be defined as licenses. Beyond these clear-cut applications of the concept, a nonprofit organization might license the use of its name on a commercial product, or a film studio might license the right to use the name of a film and/or an image on a lunch box. Nevertheless, in book publishing, the term "licensing" is usually reserved for selling the right to use an excerpt or book-derived image in a nonbook commercial product.

While most of a publisher's licensing revenue will come from such fairly predictable applications as posters, T-shirts, stationery, or mugs, occasionally licensees are rewarded with the unexpected. A stunning example came when VSI Holdings licensed the rights to design worldwide touring and permanent exhibitions based on the best-selling Grossology-themed books by science teacher Sylvia Branzei. VSI creates exhibits for display in science centers, children's museums, theme parks, malls, and zoos, and generates income through a percentage of ticket sales, further merchandising, or sponsorships. Presumably, the publisher, Penguin Putnam, would not have foreseen this use when they signed the original work in the series.

Publishers interested in licensing rights for gift products or other uses should begin with modest expectations. The process, usually handled by subrights departments at large companies, is somewhat laborious. You have to identify the properties that you think will be suitable for licensing, target the companies you think will be interested, and show them what you have in mind. In most cases it's not enough to say you think this image would look great on a T-shirt. You have to show them.

Standard contracts are similar to author contracts in that they provide for exclusive rights either worldwide or within a geographic area, an advance, royalties as a percent of net sales, and limited duration (typically three years). For publishers these deals will usually be treated as subrights with their authors, so that revenues are split.

Those interested in finding out more about the larger world of licensing can begin by contacting the International Licensing Industry Merchandisers' Association (*www.licensing.org*).

Chronicle Books Evolves from Licensor to Gift Publisher

For Chronicle Books, the immense of success of *Griffin and Sabine* and its sequels by author/illustrator Nick Bantock brought the added realization that the attractive images in these highly illustrated books could be profitably adapted for use in ancillary products. Thus came about the creation of Chronicle's gift division, specializing in such items as note cards, stationery, postcards, address books, and posters.

Over time the division came to function much like a separate licensing business with the main client being its own books. Nevertheless, Chronicle does license products from other sources and also licenses some Chronicle properties to other companies. Whether "licensing in" (buying) or "licensing out" (selling), Chronicle tries to build on its strengths as a gift publisher. Having established markets in bookstores and gift shops for certain kinds of high quality products, it looks for other images that can be adapted to these products.

Chronicle has, for instance, worked with D.C. Comics and Harley-Davidson to produce extensive lines such as those done from the *Griffin & Sabine* images. The company has also worked with Lucasfilms, producing offset litho poster reproductions of *Phantom Menace* designs by scene artist Doug Chiang, which were packaged as a set in a metal posterbox. Having the appearance of a limited edition, but priced for a mass audience, the posters were a natural fit for Chronicle's gift market.

10

Book Publicity Basics

In industries other than publishing, the epithet "public relations" often refers to a variety of functions and techniques for cultivating a favorable corporate image and a memorable presence—whether before the general public, stockholders, or legislators. In book publishing, the term is usually used synonymously with "publicity" and "media relations." Its purpose, first and foremost, is to get the attention of readers, through the media, for books on a title-by-title basis.

Often the first hire for a start-up trade publisher, sometimes even before paying himself or herself fully, is a publicist—someone to get out review copies, arrange for excerpts and articles, set up author tours, schedule interviews and booksignings, create special events, and cultivate the media. Because of the vital importance of the media in promoting and selling books, publishers are more and more concerned when signing contracts about whether authors will perform well with the media. At the same time, many authors are recognizing the need to take responsibility for marketing themselves and their own work and are either hiring publicists on their own or learning how to approach the media themselves.

These actions express and reflect three basic truths about trade publishing:

- Publicity is usually the most cost-effective marketing available
- When dealing with a diffuse audience, the general media allows you to spread your message broadly
- There are so many media outlets—both general and specialized— that almost every book and author can attract some attention

WORD-OF-MOUTH MAGIC

In survey after survey, people report that the recommendation of friends counts as one of their top reasons for choosing to buy a particular book. Just as the film industry knows that the millions of dollars it spends on advertising only starts a process in which ultimate success depends on the enjoyment of filmgoers, your public relations campaign gets the word out to your most likely prospects. If they're mildly enthusiastic about your book, they will recommend it as occasions arise. If they're wildly enthusiastic about your book, they will bend people's ears tirelessly. The publishing industry is filled with stories about books that were originally published in small print runs—with proportionately modest marketing budgets—that went on to be bestsellers because the book hit a responsive chord with readers. There are also plenty of anecdotes about books by celebrity authors—marketed with all the resources of a large company—that never earned out their huge advances.

A further point to keep in mind is that some books may be very easy to publicize while others are much more difficult, and your publicity may not produce proportionate sales. This doesn't mean you should skimp on your public relations efforts out of a cynical sense they won't pay off, but it does mean you should monitor your efforts and watch for results. Occasionally, you'll find a topic that radio interviewers love, and you can schedule your author every day of the week for weeks on end, yet the entertainment value of hearing about the book doesn't translate into sales. Conversely, there are plenty of good, solid books with a serious audience that don't offer themselves as topics for the mass media. They may get a few reviews in specialty magazines, and because members of their specialty audience communicate with each other, the books take on a life of their own.

Of course, these situations represent the exception. For the most part, media outlets both reflect and influence their audiences. Enthusiastic reviews and frequent appearances on talk shows generally produce sales—and the more you have of both the better—while authors who are tireless self-promoters generally reap the benefits in sales. Nevertheless, once the reviews have come and gone and the author has retired from the circuit to write the next book, a work either continues to sell or disappears, based on its intrinsic appeal to readers and its position in the marketplace.

Secondary Uses for Your Publicity

In addition to the sales surge and word of mouth generated by publicity, both authors and publishers should generally be aware of their opportunities to make continuing use of publicity long after it appears. When a book is reprinted, the publisher can add positive quotes from reviews to the cover, and these same quotes can be used in direct-mail promotions, backlist catalogs, and foreign rights sales. Publishers can also point to their previous record of waging successful public relations campaigns when courting new authors.

For the small or start-up publisher, there is also the critical factor of establishing credibility. I mentioned above that, among book publishers, public relations is limited to promoting individual titles, and this is true most of the time. Occasionally, however, independent publishers need some ammunition for promoting their company as a whole, and a strong portfolio of clippings can be extremely useful. A glowing profile of their operations from a business columnist, positive mentions in *Publishers Weekly*, and a sheaf of reviews can tip the balance in making a sale or negotiating a loan.

Authors, for their part, should keep a scrapbook of their clippings as well as a log of radio and television appearances, not just as a salve to their writer's ego, but to prove their marketing value when negotiating new book contracts. Good reviews, a track record of success, and the ability to market your own work are all persuasive factors to a publisher considering a new project.

A strong public relations effort pays for itself long after the initial burst has been forgotten.

TARGETING THE MEDIA

While professional publicists, whether in-house or independent, naturally have certain assumptions and routines that help them work efficiently, it may be that for you efficiency is not as important as nailing down every possibility. Or it may be that your time and budget are severely limited and you must narrow your efforts accordingly. No matter which situation applies, if you want to make the most of your opportunities to promote your books, you need to know how different outlets work and the needs of the people involved in running them. Here are some tips for maximizing your opportunities.

NEWSPAPERS

Over 1,500 daily newspapers and more than 8,000 weeklies are published in the United States—more than you could ever hope or even want to contact. While most publicists focus on the top one hundred or so dailies with circulations of one hundred thousand or more, those who are conducting what might be called a saturation campaign might also try to reach papers with circulations over fifty thousand. In developing your own strategy, you should be aware that as circulation diminishes, so does a paper's staff and editorial space. Small papers have fewer readers, and there is less opportunity for coverage within the paper. With the exception of the alternative press and other specialized publications in tabloid form—which can offer a very strong audience for certain kinds of books—most publicists ignore the weeklies altogether.

As noted previously, the most prestigious spot placement for book publishers is the book-review section of the *New York Times*. A review there can launch a book into success, even a book without highly commercial expectations. While only a few other papers have their own pull-out book-review sections (most papers feature book reviews somewhere in the paper), and for certain kinds of books—fiction and serious nonfiction, history, religion, public policy, and like topics—your goal as publicist will be to get a "traditional" book review in these columns.

There are, however, many books that are not only inappropriate for the book-review section, but would be better featured elsewhere in the paper. Real estate books, business books, cookbooks, self-help and how-to books, and sports and fitness books are all more likely to be treated in a feature article or review in one of the specialty sections of the newspaper rather than in the book-review section. As the publicist for such books, your mailings should target the editors of the appropriate sections rather than the book review. Target the appropriate special Sunday sections as well, since Sunday editions usually have a significantly higher circulation and a lot more editorial space.

For some books, when dealing with the larger papers, you may want to mail information to book-review editors and to editors of a particularly relevant section. If you do, be sure to notify these editors whether anyone else at their paper has received the story. Papers won't want to cover the book twice, and you don't want to create inadvertent ill will by leading an editor to pursue a story only to discover that a colleague has already written on the subject. You also have the option of working directly with beat reporters and columnists. While reporters usually have to clear an article with editors, and conversely are often assigned articles by an editor, columnists tend to function independently. If you don't have experience with particular writers, you should probably begin by approaching editors before you pitch reporters. You should contact columnists directly, but be sure to follow the general rule of letting them know if you have pitched a story or sent a book to someone else at the same paper.

When assembling your newspaper list, keep in mind that a few newspapers give you national coverage—USA Today, the Wall Street Journal, the Christian Science Monitor—and that these may have special value for you beyond their circulation. Sunday papers also feature inserts, such as Parade, that garner a wide audience for popular topics. On the other hand, if you are promoting a regional book, these papers may be of less interest than a small local paper that would fall below the gaze of most book publicists.

NEWS SERVICES AND SYNDICATES

Oftentimes, articles that appear in the *New York Times*, the *Washington Post*, the *Chicago Tribune*, and other major newspapers, are reprinted by various smaller papers throughout the country, so the results of your publicity are miraculously multiplied. While these can be considered unexpected gifts, there are a number of syndication and wire services that create stories for many news outlets, which you can and should target with your press materials.

The largest of these—AP, Reuters, and UPI—all have numerous local bureaus specializing in hard news, as well as editors and columnists providing material on almost any topic relevant to a newspaper. While news reporters are generally unlikely candidates to write about a book per se, if your author makes some news—through an important award, for instance, or as a commentator on a breaking story—your local bureau may well be interested. In addition, there are dozens of feature syndicates with writers on every major topic. In looking over the media directory listings for feature syndicates, this is where you find such household names as Molly Ivins, "Click and Clack" brothers, Tom and Ray Magliozzi, as well as numerous lesser lights who have a large audience nevertheless.

RADIO AND TELEVISION

Between the giant, popular, national television and radio talk and news shows viewed by millions and the tiny local broadcast in a minor market, caverns yawn. At one end is a well-staffed, high-powered, slick presentation—with a carefully designed element of spontaneity—that regularly features world-famous guests. And at the other, a host and perhaps a producer, often barely out of college, with few resources and working hard to fill airtime with interesting and entertaining shows.

Yet despite their differences, most of these shows work in similar ways, and their success relies on many of the same elements: a lively host, an articulate guest, and an interesting topic. Naturally, what constitutes an interesting topic varies from show to show, depending on the show's focus and its target audience, but with literally thousands of shows broadcast daily, there are opportunities for authors to discuss every topic imaginable and promote their books. For the publicist charged with setting up interviews, the burden is to communicate how and why a particular author would make an interesting guest through an effective press kit and telephone pitch.

For the author, the challenge is to be that interesting guest. This doesn't mean remaking yourself into a media star, but you should have a sense of how you look or sound on radio or television, and a certain degree of preparation can help. For authors just starting out, it certainly helps to do some local shows first to develop confidence, and although costly, media coaches can teach some valuable skills. Both coaches and local shows can provide videotapes of sessions, and you should be sure to get these for later use.

Read, Listen, and Watch—Be a Media Junkie

Here is one more tip, obvious in theory but difficult to implement: Try to read every publication and listen to or watch every show that might feature your author or book. Most important, familiarize yourself with the interests of as many writers and hosts as you can. When you're in a new city, pick up the local papers and go through them to see who covers what.

All of this will give you an inside edge when you are looking for coverage on a particular topic. While there are pitch books that can help you with your homework (see Resources, page 215), most media lists and directories give you names of contacts and their departments, but they won't tell you that even though a particular writer covers the education beat, she always covers adoption stories because she has a personal connection with the topic. If you happen to know this because you've read the articles, you have an opening for a story on your adoption book.

Researching the Right Media for Your Book

Years ago, I took a course in public relations, and at the first meeting, the instructor walked in with a stationery box filled with press releases. She held them up before the class and said, "Imagine that I'm an editor or producer, and these are the press releases I received today. How do I choose a topic to pursue from among them? And how do you get me interested in your message?" She responded to her own query by saying, "When I read through this pile of paper I ask myself two questions, 'Why me, and why now?' These are the points you have to address."

Not only was her simple demonstration memorable, but it offers a valuable insight into creating an effective publicity strategy. As with any form of sales, you can't really convince someone to buy something they don't want. You need to find the most responsive audience available and present what you have in the strongest way you can. At the core of your strategy, however, should be a good understanding of what editors, reporters, or producers are looking for and what they need. They have a certain job to do. They are looking for material all the time, and you can help—if your story is right for them.

If, for instance, you have written or published an introduction to investing for novices, your media audience may include a large selection of talk show hosts, general consumer magazines, and newspapers. In contrast, if you are promoting an extremely technical work on the analysis of derivatives that will be understandable only to financial professionals, the radio talk show circuit would be an inefficient use of your time. Producers and hosts won't particularly want you as a guest, and even if you could speak in a general way to their listeners, you wouldn't be selling books. A more efficient route to your target audience would probably be through specialty newsletters and journals for financial professionals, high-end business magazines, and a targeted newspaper such as the *Wall Street Journal*.

As with direct mail, building your list—in this case your media list—is the basis for developing an effective public relations effort. Also as with direct mail, if you are a niche publisher, your efforts will be much more productive. You will benefit by establishing relationships with editors and producers with whom you work regularly, you can keep track of them as they move from post to post—a common occurrence among media professionals—and you will be a resource for them when they are looking for information or someone to interview in your field of expertise.

Of course, there will always be titles, even on the most tightly focused lists, that will force you to look farther afield than your established contacts, and this is where you will be called upon to use your imagination and do a little exploring.

Finding an Audience for a Do-It-Yourself Patent Book

Years ago I was called upon by Nolo Press to publicize a massive paperback volume entitled *Patent It Yourself*. Lacking any relevant background that would help me understand either the book or its audience, my first response was to get in touch with the author and ask him about who would use his book and how. In fact, he had quite clear ideas on the subject.

As a patent attorney with an engineering background, he explained that engineers in all kinds of specialties deal with patent issues all the time. Of course, large corporations that had their own attorneys wouldn't want the book, but there were plenty of independent contractors who wanted to patent their inventions and plenty of staff people who worked after hours on their own projects who would also want the book. On the basis of this information, I concluded that the established Nolo Press media list of reporters, editors, and talk show hosts interested in consumer issues would find the book of little interest.

I needed a whole new media list—one that featured publications directed to engineers. I went to the library and started hand compiling a list of hundreds of technical publications from magazine and newsletter directories. As opposed to the usual trade-oriented material I was used to promoting, my concern here was not with the circulation size of any particular journal or magazine, but whether they reviewed books and whether their readers would be involved in research and development work. Even a small newsletter would do if it seemed to have the right focus. Again, lacking any real knowledge of the fields I was researching, I didn't try to assemble a tight, efficient list. I simply thumbed through the directories looking for technical categories, and every time I saw the words

---

"research," "development," or "engineering," I pounced. I also found, much to my amazement, a group of publications specifically for inventors.

Back in the office, I assembled a fairly large and expensive mailing of review copies and then held my breath to see if I would get any results. In fact, to my pleasure and amazement, reviews started coming in—dozens of glowing reviews. I had probably mailed to all kinds of publications for whom the book was inappropriate, but it really didn't matter, because the many positive reviews helped establish the book as a primary resource for a very specialized audience.

At this point—even with solid success in getting positive reviews—I still treated the book as some weird anomaly. I still had another lesson to learn about the mystery of what makes a story and what sells. A few months after publication, the author—among my least likely candidates for media star—approached me and asked me to book him on Larry King's late-night national radio show. He was going to be on the East Coast for business, he said, and since his topic was a natural for the show, I should arrange an interview. After all, he continued, inventors work late at night and listen to the radio.

I was taken aback. I certainly didn't want to embarrass myself by pitching this book and its nerdy author to one of America's favorite talk show-hosts, but I couldn't very well say no. To make a long story short, Larry King ended up doing a lengthy interview with the author and even gave our toll-free phone number. The next day the phone rang off the hook with orders. End of story? No. A few months later, while King was on vacation, the interview was rebroadcast, and we got a second flood of direct orders.

THE COMPLEMENTARY ROLES OF PRINT AND ELECTRONIC MEDIA

The public relations campaign for *Patent It Yourself* described above, not only taught me a bit of humility and something about how to find a technical audience, but also that a book I assumed would be suitable only for print coverage could also be successfully presented on talk radio. Over the years, this lesson has been reinforced again and again, and I have come to understand—along with most book publicists— that the radio interview is a remarkably powerful vehicle for promoting books of all kinds.

Not only are there thousands of local radio shows that conduct phone interviews and have time slots to fill, these programs feature an incredible range of topics. They also tend to cover a topic in considerable depth, with interviews commonly running from fifteen minutes to a half hour. With a segment of this length, authors can provide a significant amount of information about their books. They can mention the title repeatedly and, when the host is amenable, give ordering information.

In contrast, four minutes on television is usually considered an eternity, and while a local television talk show will often display a book's cover and mention that the book is available in local bookstores, these television appearances are often less effective at promoting a book than their radio equivalents. Whether this is the result of the short segment or the demographics is hard to say, and I have never seen any research to verify these observations. In saying this, I am not suggesting that a publicist or author should ignore the opportunities afforded by television appearances. I am merely pointing out that, contrary to common expectations, a local television appearance is not necessarily more valuable than a local radio interview. Radio and television should be pursued with equal vigor.

There are, of course, the major national television shows, and probably no one in the history of the world has been as effective at selling books as Oprah, even before her book club. For an author to score an appearance on either this show or one of the competing national talk or news shows is akin to entering the Promised Land. The audiences for these shows are huge, and they buy books. In addition, having appeared on one of these shows, an author suddenly becomes more in demand among local media. Naturally, the producers for these shows have their pick of authors and topics—and they have a very firm sense of what works and doesn't work on their shows—so unless you're pitching a celebrity author, you have an uphill battle in booking an interview. You can't make these shows central to your publicity plans, even with a dynamic author, a strong book, and a timely topic, but if you're lucky enough to schedule an appearance, you'll see the results on your sales. If not, there is still a multitude of shows with a book-buying audience that will want to hear about your topic.

As with radio and television, there are thousands of newspapers, magazines, journals, and newsletters, both local and national, with readerships that range from a handful of specialists to a vast national audience. In developing a publicity strategy, your first job is to sort through these to find which are the most likely candidates to take an interest. While in most cases you will pitch both print and electronic media, this may not always be possible. Perhaps you don't have an author available to do interviews, so that print media coverage becomes even more important, or perhaps you have a book, even more technical than *Patent It Yourself*, that truly does not lend itself to radio or television.

One point to keep in mind is that while radio and television stations and newspapers may all share a specific market, they are usually open to covering the same book and the same author. If you do manage to secure publicity in several different outlets, you'll find the overlapping coverage increases sales geometrically. Conflicts may occur, however, between two radio stations in the same market, or two television stations, or two newspapers. So, when booking a market new to you, be sure to confirm whether a station or publication requires either exclusivity or first exposure.

Also keep in mind that while print reviews of a book can be useful and persuasive in pitching an author to a radio or television producer, producers and hosts are neither impressed nor interested in hearing about all the other talk shows an author has done, especially if they are in nearby markets. Similarly, no editor or writer wants to be the last one to have covered a story. While a glowing review from the *New York Times* may lead writers elsewhere in the country to pursue an article—"qualifying" an author or story in much the same way an appearance on Oprah does—you won't advance your cause with newspaper editors by pointing out that ten other newspapers in your state have given your book glowing reviews. Instead, you're telling them that the story is old.

CREATING AND NURTURING YOUR MEDIA LIST

Earlier in this chapter, I described how I assembled a list of technical publications from various directories for publicizing a do-it-yourself patent book. I also alluded to the fact that I maintained a list of media contacts who were consistently interested in the kinds of issues usually treated in Nolo Press books—reporters who specialized in consumer issues, self-help advocates, business writers with an interest in legal issues, and so forth.

Over the years, I had sent these people material and spoken to them on the phone. I knew their interests and their professional needs, and when we had a new title on business, real estate, or family law, I knew which people would be particularly interested. I would send them books, make follow-up calls, and work with them to provide any extra information they needed. I would, of course, send books to other members of my list as well, and I was always looking for new contacts, but I paid special interest to a core list, with whom I worked closely.

The best part of this situation was that I became a resource for these contacts just as they had become a resource for me. Sometimes, in fact, they would call me with a particular request—a guest had canceled and they needed someone to fill in at the last moment, or they needed a quote on a particular subject—and I could steer them to one of our authors. While this was the system working at its best, I should point out that my situation was not unique. An in-house publicist working with a niche publisher can and should develop working relationships with the media people who cover the publisher's area of expertise, and these relationships benefit all involved.

If you are new to the field, you'll have to begin by creating your own media list. You can use the library to do your initial research, or you can buy media contact directories or electronic databases. The latter may be too expensive for authors or self-publishers whose public relations efforts will be limited to a few campaigns a year, but they will be a solid investment for any publisher that plans on building an in-house public relations function.

Whichever path you choose, your immediate aim will be to create a computer database that includes contact information—name, institution, street address, phone and fax numbers, and e-mail address—as well as sort fields for areas of interest, media type, and geographical location. Your database should also have a field for additional notes, which you can use to remind yourself of particular conversations with your contacts. Using this database, you will want to be able to generate customized mailing lists, labels, and reports. You will probably want the ability to export data as well, so that you can create mail-merged cover letters, faxes, and e-mail messages.

When planning a campaign, this list will be your first stop and last resort. You will want to go through your contacts to see who should receive a book and/or press kit. You may also want to go to the media directories or databases to see if there are any categories you should add to your database for the title at hand. Determining the appropriate media for your campaign is usually extremely helpful in clarifying your approach.

Because media people are constantly moving from one job to another within the industry, keeping your list up to date is an important chore. The directory and database publishers listed at the end of this chapter offer their products as serials—you can subscribe, and they will send you updates—or as onetime purchases. Choosing between these two options will depend on your budget, your time, and how you use lists. If you maintain regular contact with a small group of media people, you can make your own changes and enter updates with each round of mailings and follow-up calls. If, on the other hand, you find yourself pursuing many different categories of media contacts over the course of a year and from year to year, you may want to pay extra and have current contact information.

How to Adjust the Scope of Your Campaign

Each year, a few notable authors from the largest publishers are treated to the all-out author's tour. Complete with escort services, first-class hotels, and fancy restaurants, these privileged authors find themselves whirling from city to city, studio to studio, and bookstore to bookstore. Clearly, the expense of such treatment is justified only when you're projecting huge sales. Nevertheless, a lot can be done within the constraints of limited finances, and a strong public relations campaign can be run on a limited budget.

In fact, the largest expense in a public relations campaign is in the labor, whether as a staff person or an independent contractor. Those who choose to do the job themselves can limit their expenses to the cost of the books, shipping or mailing costs, some duplicating charges, and telephone expenses. In either case, when you have a book that you expect to sell primarily through bookstores, publicity is both your primary tool and the most cost-effective method for moving those books from the store shelves into the hands of readers.

Given these facts, it makes sense to conduct as strong a public relations campaign as possible. Naturally, you need to take into account your reasonable expectations for a particular book and not overspend, but in your marketing and financial planning, you should have budgeted enough to get the word out to your potential readers.

PRINT MEDIA FIRST

As a rule of thumb, I usually tell publishers that the cheapest item in their marketing budget are the books they send out for review, and that they should begin a public relations campaign by assembling a print review list. There is a threefold strategy here: Print reviews are effective at getting word of mouth going among actual readers; they provide material for further promotions, as mentioned above; and they give cost-effective national coverage. Depending on the book, you can pull a list of book-review editors at large circulation newspapers in all the major markets defined geographically, or you can compile a list of technical publications—as with the *Patent It Yourself* example—that will be read by your target audience wherever they happen to live and work.

I counsel those who are new to this process to be as thorough as possible and track down as many editors and writers as they think would be legitimately interested in a book. If you find your list expanding way beyond the number of books budgeted for review, you can prioritize your mailing, sending books only to the most important publications. To publications that are merely potentially interested, or with which you are unfamiliar, you can send a press release with a self-addressed postcard to be used for requesting a review copy. Be sure to include a space for the person's phone number, so you can follow up with a phone call.

HOME-BASED PUBLICITY

If, as a publisher, you can't afford to pay for travel, but you have an author who speaks well and is articulate in presenting his work, you can take advantage of these qualities by promoting radio phone interviews. These can be done any day of the week and any hour of the day. They can be done from the kitchen in your bathrobe and, in fact, often are. And while it doesn't matter if you live in Los Angeles or Duluth, authors need to develop the resilience to answer questions from pumped-up, drive-time deejays in different time zones. The wonder of this medium is that authors can present their work in every small town and large city in the country. They can answer their readers' questions directly, present their points of view, and promote their books with all the enthusiasm and wit at their command. Such programs were made for a topic with broad popular appeal, and the medium is perfect for reaching a geographically diffuse and diverse audience.

REGIONAL CAMPAIGNING HAS A PLACE

For authors who live in or near major metropolitan areas, it's also worthwhile to set up regional events. Local bookstores are apprecia-tive of the attention, and local newspapers want to provide coverage of a local author. Regional campaigns are also a good starting point for authors and/or publishers with limited budgets who want to gauge a book's potential before investing further time and money.

If audiences respond with enthusiasm and bookstores reorder more than once, you can assume that your publicity has been effective and the book is getting positive word of mouth. You can then make some projections to determine whether you will sell enough books to justify the cost of travel.

This is an area where publishers and authors can work together creatively. Perhaps an author has friends or family with whom he can stay in a distant city and is willing to share travel costs with his pub-lisher, if the publisher can make the media contacts and set up events. Or perhaps an author travels frequently on business and is willing to extend her stay to do some media events arranged by the publisher. Regional campaigns can be extended city by city as an author's time and a publisher's resources allow.

How to Promote a Coffee Table Book

Illustrated gift books, coffee table books, and other kinds of highly visual or inspirational works are often excluded from conventional media coverage. There's little opportunity for talk show appearances, and book reviewers ordinarily want to discuss some kind of substantive text, not describe pictures. There are, however, effective of ways to promote these books. It just takes a little more effort and imagination to craft a workable plan.

A good place to begin is by looking within the book itself for promotion ideas. The experience of Westcliffe Publishers with its book, *Oregon: Then & Now,* presents a good example. Matching contemporary photography with historic photographs and essays, the volume combines a strong regional appeal, a "story" embedded in the comparison of old and new photos of the same places, plus a text that pulls the book's images together. A seemingly obvious promotional possibility, and one that has proved successful, has been to send copies of photos to small regional newspapers throughout the state featuring sites within their particular circulation areas.

Supplementing these efforts, the publisher contacted art galleries and set up shows throughout the state. In addition, some of the book's collaborators toured the state with a slideshow. They took the show to bookstores, the state historical society, shopping malls, colleges, and the "Made in Oregon" chain retailer.

The success of these promotions clearly offers a model for gift books of all sorts. Whether your book features photos of peregrine falcons, Turkish villages, or baseball memorabilia, there are ways to promote the book through the material. You can target a specialty or niche audience, find periodicals that will feature illustrations drawn from the book, and locate venues to display original art and host events.

TIME IS MORE THAN MONEY

While in the past it was important to get publicity for a book soon after it hit the shelf, now timing is critical. Just-in-time inventory has meant not only that bookstores order and stock fewer copies of frontlist titles, but that books are being returned sooner. Your window of opportunity to establish a pattern of sales in the trade has narrowed, and the sad fact is that if your publicity hits after your books have been returned, your efforts have been mostly wasted.

At the front end of the cycle, the value of any publicity you receive before a book hits the shelf is also greatly depleted. As a consumer, if I go into a bookstore to buy a book I just heard about on the radio, I want the book then and there. That's why I am in the store. If the book isn't there, unless I have an unusually strong interest in that particular title, I'll probably just purchase something else. By the following week, when the book has arrived, I'll have read five more reviews and heard another ten authors on the air, and I'll be looking for these books, not the book I heard about the week before.

Presumably, the growth of online sales will help publishers overcome some of these problems. Books are now easily accessible to consumers even when they're not on bookstore shelves, and people who order online are used to waiting for a book to ship. Effective publicity should create sales through all your channels—bookstores, nonbook retailers, direct mail, and online—many of which are less sensitive to time. Nevertheless, if the bookstore is a major source of your revenue, the timing of your publicity will be critical to your success.

YEAR-ROUND PUBLIC RELATIONS

In contrast to the initial publicity campaign for a new book, those who are building backlist sales, whatever their channels, need not look upon their efforts at publicity as a single, time-limited event that coincides with a book's publication. Authors who are engaged with their topics as speakers or consultants can use every engagement as an opportunity both to sell books directly and to promote public awareness of their work.

Books that treat subjects of perennial interest and continue to be stocked as backlist items in stores can continue to draw media attention. The trick is to present the book and author in the right way. Because a book isn't new doesn't mean you can't publicize it. If I, as a producer, host, or member of the audience, haven't heard about the book before, or if I don't know about something the book explains, then it's new to me and it's news to me. Here, again, radio works well.

While magazines and newspapers tend to emphasize newness, radio hosts are looking for interesting guests to fill airtime.

While some subjects and some books are timeless and can be promoted any time of the year, others can be tied to current events or seasonal holidays. A book about personal relationships, for instance, may generate interest any time, but it can also be pitched to coincide with Valentine's Day. Similarly, a book on fathering may be relevant every day of the year, but most media outlets will be looking for material for a Father's Day story. It may be that the publication of your fathering book is timed to take advantage of this need, and perhaps you will succeed in getting a good publicity hit, but why stop there? If, a year later, your book is still available and selling, you can repeat your public relations efforts with excellent if not equal results. Moreover, you can make the holiday an annual event on your promotions calendar as long as the book is available and as long as you have the energy.

YEAR-ROUND WRITING TO PROMOTE YOUR BOOK

Just as an author of a fathering book can do yearly radio interviews for Father's Day, he can also offer an article on fathering, or a series of articles, to magazines and newspapers each year. Such an article might do well on the op-ed (opposite editorial) pages of newspapers or in the many regional parenting publications.

While the holiday hook works well with such articles, the author who is regularly engaged in writing and speaking about a particular topic can continue to generate original or derivative articles year-round. And while you cannot always reference your own book in these articles, your credit line can identify you as the author of such-and-such book. Authors who are active commentators on a particular topic sell more books and increase their value as authors.

11

Creating an Effective PR Campaign

As with most activities, your public relations efforts will improve as you become more experienced. Whether you're doing this work as a publisher, an author, or a staff publicist, the process is the same. You learn how to work with different media outlets—who to contact, what they need, how to time your pitch—and you begin to cultivate specific communication skills, both in your written pieces and in your telephone work. You will also get to know, even if just through brief phone conversations, an expanding group of editors, reporters, producers, and hosts. As a publicist, these relationships are your equity. The wider your circle of contacts, the easier your job becomes, and, over time, the more successful you will be.

CHOOSING YOUR PITCH—SELLING THE STORY VERSUS SELLING THE BOOK

The simple fact that a book is newly published doesn't make it news. To turn the publication of a book into a newsworthy item, you need a hook on which you can hang a story—something that people will want to talk, hear, and read about. Before approaching a radio producer or a newspaper editor, you, as publicist, publisher, or author, need to distill the "story" from the book. In other words, you need to find or invent the angle that turns a static book into a dynamic topic for discussion.

There are several common methods for doing this: You can personalize your topic through an illustrative anecdote, you can focus on one especially dramatic example from the book, or you can simply emphasize a thread from the book that connects to a topic of current concern. The critical issue is to look beyond the book you're promoting to the needs and interests of media people, and give them a story they can use.

Invent a Word, Sell a Book

The marketing staff of Conari Press clearly understood the need for a media hook when they developed their public relations plans for their hit title, *Sheroes,* by Varla Ventura. Having already enjoyed success with the press's Wild Women Series and its "fun feminism," they saw the trick was to find a way to tell the media that their new book was more than just another collection of anecdotal biographies of notable women.

Recognizing that the strength of the book, as well as its challenge, was in the title, they decided to make the word "shero" the central focus of their pitch. In their media kit they emphasized that the word filled a need among women today, declaring that "women of courage must have a name of their own." They also initiated a drive to have "shero" included in the eleventh edition of *Merriam-Webster's Collegiate Dictionary.* To encourage and engage their readers in this drive, Conari included both a sample letter to the dictionary's editors in the back of the book, as well as a form for readers to submit their own favorite sheroes for inclusion in later editions.

Conari's no-holds-barred cover copy and promotional materials fairly shout the message, proclaiming that the word evokes "fiery fempower . . . from the sheroic foremothers who blazed trails and broke barriers, to today's women warriors from sports, science,

---

cyberspace, city hall, the lecture hall, and the silver screen." With a cover sporting photos of Anita Hill as well as television sheroes agent Dana Scully and Xena, Conari extols the "Bold, Brash (and Absolutely Unabashed) Superwomen" of this book.

To reinforce its promotional efforts, the book's publication was scheduled to coincide with the 150th anniversary celebration of the Seneca Falls suffragette convention, credited with launching the women's movement. Conari arranged to have the book featured at the bookstore attached to the celebration—an event attended by Hillary Rodham Clinton and Judy Collins, among other notables— and made the celebration the first stop on a six-city author tour during which the author stayed with friends. Bookstore signings— mixing chains and independents—were scheduled for each of these cities, and as a promotional gimmick stores were given packs of free trading cards featuring ten sheroes from the book, including Jane Fonda as Barbarella, Betty Friedan, and Marie Curie.

While pitching editors and producers with the serious message that today's girls and women need daring role models, Conari emulated the fun and feisty nature of the book by offering a list of sheroes that places Tina Turner next to Eleanor Roosevelt and Miss Marple next to Sally Ride.

The results of this campaign were spectacular, with over seventy forthcoming interviews and reviews, including coverage in *Glamour, Billboard*, the *Los Angeles Times*, and the *Chicago Tribune*. The author appeared on the *Laurie Lee Show*, Lifetime TV, the CBC, and even the *Voice of America*, as well as numerous regional radio and television shows.

While publishers and publicists might look on such results with envy, it's important to keep in mind that they were not the product of a high-budget marketing campaign. The key to Conari's success in promoting this title was to see the book's strengths and present them in a way that the story told itself.

TIMING YOUR PITCH

Because the window of opportunity in the trade is so narrow, most publishers and publicists work on tight schedules to get their publicity going. They can't get the story out too early or too late, and so they must time their pitch to take into account the lead times required by the various media with whom they're dealing.

Daily newspapers, for instance, usually follow up on a story immediately. Nevertheless, certain departments within a paper may have longer lead times. Feature and style editors might be working on a story a week ahead of when it appears, while a Sunday real-estate section, for instance, might work several weeks ahead. Papers with pull-out book-review sections might work several months ahead, because they have to assign reviews, send out the books, wait for the reviews to arrive, and still have the reviews coincide with the publication dates.

Similarly, radio and television hosts typically book guests anywhere from one to three weeks ahead, but sometimes they scramble to fill a slot when a guest suddenly has a change of plans. When dealing with these media, you should also be aware that a breaking news story could preempt your appearance.

At the other end of the time spectrum from newspapers are the monthly magazines that set their editorial schedules a year in advance. Obviously, you're not working that far ahead, but you need to send galleys to book reviewers in these publications as early as you can, hopefully three or four months before publication. If, instead of a review, you are looking to place an excerpt or sell an original article to coincide with publication, you probably need six months or more of leadtime.

THE PHONE PITCH

The ideal procedure for running a public relations campaign is usually summed up as such: phone, mail, phone. That is, phone first to make an initial contact, determine the right person to receive your materials, and when appropriate, give a quick pitch. Second, mail your press materials. Finally, follow up with a phone call to confirm receipt and give your pitch for a booking or article. Rarely, however, do publicists have time for all these stages. When time is limited, they will generally omit the first call and rely on the accuracy of their list and the power of their press materials to make the first pitch. When dealing with a breaking story where snail mail will have missed the window of opportunity, they may just call, fax, or e-mail.

Such tactics should not be abused, however. The first rule in doing phone work with media people is to respect their time. Like everyone else in the modern world, they are being asked to do too much in too little time. In addition, they are constantly dealing with deadlines that can't be fudged. If they are preparing for a show that goes on in an hour or completing an article that goes to press before lunch, they don't want to talk, and they will resent your intrusion. So, when calling, be sure to ask if this is a good time to talk. Then be prepared to make your pitch clearly and succinctly.

THE SEVEN-WORD PITCH

As with a piece of writing, the first sentence of your phone pitch is the most important in capturing the interest and attention of your listener. More focused than an article or short story, however, your phone pitch should express the essence of the book in one sentence. I usually call this the seven-word test, though there is no magic in the number seven. It could be six or five or eight, but the shorter the better.

In formulating your pitch, try to imagine that someone has asked you: "What is this book about?" or "What does this author have to say?" Imagine as well that you have only one declarative sentence (without clauses) in which to answer them. Your answer should look like one of these:

- This book shows how Chinese herbs can prolong your life.
- Jane Author gives six clear rules for winning at office politics.
- *Sheroes* offers women two hundred models of courage.

You don't want to say something like, "For over thousands of years, Chinese medical practitioners have developed a system of medical wisdom that delineates this and that and so forth." This might be okay for your second or third sentence, but the first sentence needs to define the topic and tell the producer what you are offering. If the show doesn't cover health topics, the producer doesn't need to hear more about the first book. She'll say so, and you can thank her for her time and move on.

If, on the other hand, you reach a show that often covers "work-life" issues with the second example, then your opening line should produce the response, "Tell me more." Now you move to the twenty-one–word pitch. This too is not a lot of words. Make it to the point and try to offer a choice tidbit.

"People fail at work because they don't recognize certain unspoken clues—who the boss relies on for information and how budget decisions are made. Jane Author shows how to use this information to your advantage."

Actually, I've just used thirty-five words, but at this point I should have an interested producer or editor who will probably want to know about the author's qualifications and/or how skilled this person is on the air.

FURTHER RULES FOR EFFECTIVE PHONE WORK

If, having heard my pitch, the person at the other end says, "Sorry, I don't think this one is right for me," I don't argue, and I don't try to talk him into it. I do, however, take the opportunity to ask him who else at his station or publication might be appropriate for my story. Sometimes the second or third person along the line will pick up the story, but even if not, I have the opportunity to add a couple of names to my list and make valuable contacts.

I also take a moment to ask him about what kind of stories he is interested in and would like to hear about. If he has a moment and is willing to talk, you can also take this opportunity to tell him about your line of books. He just might express interest in a recent backlist title, or even better, one of your forthcoming titles. Now you have someone asking for a book instead of rejecting your pleas. Send the book when it comes out, and include a personal note reminding him of your conversation. This is how you build relationships.

Remember that a pleasant and effective phone manner—a light touch and a sense of humor—will create opportunities, and even where nothing is forthcoming, will at least open the door for future contacts. To this I would add that it really helps if you are honestly interested in what your media contacts are doing. Like you, they are people at a job, and like you, they probably don't get enough appreciation. Your interest and your care counts.

HIRING A PUBLICIST

For trade publishers with a steady flow of new titles, having a staff publicist is a good investment. Working in-house, a publicist can develop relationships with regular contacts, and even if the publicist leaves, the contact list remains with the publisher. In addition, the in-house publicist can develop procedures for pitching an entire season's publications while supporting backlist titles and authors as opportunities arise. I strongly recommend this path for those who have the volume of business to support such efforts.

Nevertheless, many freelance publicists and agencies have the advantage of long experience and good contacts, so that when they are pitching a book for you, they can be very focused and effective. For many publishers, and increasingly for authors, contracting these services works out well.

If you are considering hiring a freelance publicist, my first suggestion is to look for someone with specific experience as a book publicist. Others can do the job, but they tend to be more expensive while at the same time being unfamiliar with the language and conventions of publishing. Those who do book publicity exclusively should already have cultivated appropriate media lists and know what constitutes a good press kit to represent an author and book. While good publicists can be expensive, those who do their job well are worth the price. They work hard, and though results are never guaranteed, they earn their fees.

Most are used to working on a city-by-city basis for author tours, charging a set amount per city, and can quote a price for a full publicity campaign, including mailing to print media. When negotiating with a publicist, be sure to determine the level of follow-up included in the price, the kind of reports you will be given, and whether the publicist subscribes to a clipping service.

In addition to the conventional publicist services described above, there are certain publicity services that charge on a per-placement basis. In other words, they have a set fee for every interview or article they actually obtain for you. While an arrangement in which you only pay for results may be tempting, I suggest that you carefully calculate what your results are really worth before contracting with these services. In general, before investing in a publicity campaign, I want a fairly significant amount of coverage—an amount that would be less expensive under conventional billing methods. If I don't expect that amount, I would carefully question the entire effort.

For those who want to pursue the possibility of working with a public relations professional and don't know any, I suggest you begin by asking colleagues for recommendations. If, however, you are new to the business or are working in an area without a network of contacts, then I recommend two organizations that can provide referrals:

- Northern California Book Publicity and Marketing Association, P.O. Box 192803, San Francisco, CA 94119-2803
- Publishers' Publicity Association, c/o David Thalberg, Planned Television Arts, 301 East 57th Street, New York, NY 10022; Tel. (212) 593-5875

WORKING WITH A MEDIA COACH

While the services of a media coach are expensive, for authors who want to maximize the exposure of their books through public events, television, and radio, the investment can be worthwhile. And while this is an expense usually borne by authors themselves, publishers can encourage their authors to make use of these services or develop policies in which they share some of the expense.

Bookstores report that when an author has made an effective presentation, the positive impressions left on patrons and bookstore personnel contribute to extra sales for up to six months after an event. Similarly, the sales generated by radio and television interviews will reflect the skill of an author "on air." Media-skilled authors have the additional advantage of frequently being invited back to shows when they have been stimulating guests, thus generating extra promotional opportunities.

Especially relevant for authors who are shy or somewhat frightened—and a television studio can be intimidating for anyone without previous experience—a media coach can not only help you relax and enjoy being in front of an audience, but develop some important presentation skills. Getting some practice in front of a camera will help build your confidence, while a coach can help you with the way you use your voice, with your hand language and body posture, with the timing and clarity of your presentation, and tell you if you are making the points that really matter.

At the very minimum, it's important for authors presenting their work to get some feedback on how they articulate. Mumbling in front of an audience or on air will lose a lot of potential sales. Authors should also know how to turn a question around, how to work in the name of their book, and even how to deal with the occasional hostile questioner.

A good media coach can help you with all of these and, in addition, will help you develop an approach to presenting your material. Before going to an interview or public event, you should have clearly in mind ten points you want to make about your book. You should have these prioritized and practice repeating them out loud. Since you probably won't have a chance to make all ten points, you should be clear about the top five, the top three, and your single most important message. It may be you go to a television interview only to find yourself on a panel, and you only get time for that one most important point. You need to know how to make that point clearly and energetically.

TIPS TO AUTHORS FOR EFFECTIVE BOOKSTORE APPEARANCES

Having accompanied a great many authors, well-known and less well-known, on their Bay Area appearances, media escort Kathi Kamen Goldmark has developed a set of ten guidelines for helping her clients. I include them here because I couldn't do better, and frankly, every author should read them before going out to promote a book.

1. If a lot of people show up, be gracious and make eye contact with everyone on line, but help the staff keep things moving. It's bad form to complain about too many people—most of them would love to have your problem.
2. If no, or very few, people show up, try to look like you're having fun anyway. Sign stock, look busy, chat with the store employees. If you sit there looking depressed and miserable, no one will want to talk to you.

3. Remember that you have a lifelong relationship with books, writing, and bookstores. It doesn't matter how many books you sell on a given night. What matters is that booksellers are on the front lines of the industry. You are contributing to a valuable community resource. If they like you, they will sell your books for years and years to come.

4. When reading, pick a passage that's short and entertaining. It doesn't have to be your best writing—pick something that reads well out loud. Reading is a performance. Practice in front of your friends, and read out loud to yourself. If you have to, get "intensive karaoke bar training" to learn how to use a microphone and perform in front of people. Don't go on too long, or people will feel like they've heard the whole book and won't buy a copy.

5. If a really small group shows up, make the event informal. Sit in a circle and talk. Half the people there will be aspiring writers. You can bet on it! Ask them about their work.

6. Be honest and funny about being nervous.

7. Don't drink alcohol until after the reading.

8. If your sales reps show up and you have the time, invite them out for a drink or a snack after the reading.

9. When you get home, send thank-you notes to the booksellers.

10. If a bookseller offers you a book to take home, don't pick the most expensive one in the store. It will really embarrass your escort!

(Reproduced with permission of Kathi Kamen Goldmark, Goldmark Media Escorts)

BEYOND THE AUTHOR READING—CUSTOMIZING EVENTS THAT GROW FROM YOUR TITLE

When you're promoting a popular author, bookstore readings and signings are an obvious and successful method for engaging store personnel and reaching the public. The author provides the focus and attracts the audience. But how do you promote instructional materials, guidebooks, and other kinds of text-based works that are written by staff editors instead of an identifiable author?

For Berlitz International Publishing, some imaginative thinking has turned the problem of "authorless" works into a golden opportunity for widespread promotions. Looking for ways to promote the Berlitz Kids™ Language Packs, as well as other children's language instructional materials, the Berlitz staff hit upon the idea of conducting children's French and Spanish language learning events in bookstores.

Conceived as free introductory workshops for five- to nine-year-old children and their parents, the events are taught by experienced staff drawn from Berlitz's nationwide language centers. The sessions are one hour long and designed around a structured lesson plan that gives children some easy phrases and vocabulary in the language targeted for that workshop. By the end of a session, children are able to introduce themselves and say a few words.

The material in these workshops mirrors the contents of the language packs, which contain a storybook, audiocassette, picture dictionary, flash cards, a full copy of *Help Your Child with a Foreign Language*, by Opal Dunn, and a certificate of accomplishment. The hope is not only to create some buyers for this complex and unusual package, but also that bookstores will become more enthusiastic about selling Berlitz Kids titles. Berlitz, of course, also reaps the secondary benefit of increased awareness for their proprietary programs.

Aiming to develop a series of events that can be reproduced by chain and independent stores in any of the sixty-five metropolitan areas with Berlitz language centers, the company has carefully constructed an attractive event kit that contains both workshop materials and aids for promoting the events. Stores are given sign-up sheets, press releases, advertising slicks and posters, as well as a set of tips for promoting and preparing the event. The latter, in fact, provides an overview of all the elements that make up proper event planning. Structured around a timeline that begins six weeks prior to the event, store managers are instructed to place product orders—a toll-free number is given—and send out their customized press release to local media. Over the ensuing weeks they are then reminded to check inventory, send out invitations, display posters and products, and make sign-up sheets available.

On the day of the event, stores are encouraged to decorate with colored balloons that have the color names in French or Spanish written on with a magic marker. For use at the events themselves, stores are provided with name tags in French and Spanish, a colorful set of flash cards, finger puppet cutouts, a letter to parents, and an award-style certificate of participation for the children. The event-tips sheet also reminds personnel to stock a supply of scissors and tape for use in assembling the finger puppets.

The extent to which the program can be rolled out is dependent on the locations of the Berlitz centers in the sixty-five major metropolitan areas, but the potential for this program extends far beyond the capacities of even the most energetic authors to promote their work.

GOING ONLINE WITH YOUR PR EFFORTS

For publishers and publicists who are willing to go the extra mile, online efforts can reap big rewards. After all, more people are now looking to the Web for news and information of all sorts, and once there they are a few clicks away from placing an order.

That certainly was the thinking at the Horn Group, a public relations firm specializing in high-tech, when it was handed the assignment of promoting *The Gorilla Game: An Investor's Guide to Picking Winners in High Technology*, by Geoffrey A. Moore, Paul Johnson, and Tom Kippola (HarperBusiness). Staff members defined four target audiences: high-tech management teams, high-tech financial professionals, low-tech financial professionals, and semi-pro or serious amateur investors. They knew they could reach the first three groups through trade and industry specific publications, which they pitched with a conventional press kit.

To reach the fourth group, the investors themselves, required a broader approach that included the mainstream press and the World Wide Web. Knowing that "high-tech investment means an online audience," they began a laborious process of examining investment Web sites one by one looking for placement opportunities. Where they saw the possibility of coverage they contacted Webmasters and editors by phone or e-mail and pitched them.

The results were impressive. Thirty-one sites gave the book attention, including the Motley Fool and the *New York Times* Online. While a few sites simply posted a blurb about the book, others devoted space to a full review, and The Motley Fool actually did a several part interview with the author. Though it's impossible to separate the Web-based elements from the other components in measuring the results, the company states with pride that as a result of the entire campaign the book landed at number three on *Business Week*'s Bestseller list.

Distinguishing themselves from the Horn Group and most other publicists who look for supplemental coverage online, the Tenagra Corporation devotes itself exclusively to online efforts and serves such major clients as Random House, Wiley, and IDG.

The Tenagra Group also distinguishes itself by promoting clients' books to Usenet discussion groups, Internet mailing lists, and the commercial sites such as America Online, Compuserve, and Prodigy. In an effort that more resembles direct marketing than media-oriented public relations Tenagra creates a "giveaway file," usually an excerpt from the book it is promoting along with marketing copy, a tour schedule when available, and ordering information.

Once the giveaway file is ready, Tenagra posts notices to relevant groups and mailing lists announcing the availability of the excerpt. For instance, when promoting children's books for Random House—including the Magic Tree House series, the Junie B. Jones series, and the A to Z Mystery series—Tenagra searched out newsgroups serving teachers, parents and homeschooling advocates, and mailing lists concerned with children's literature. In its postings, Tenagra is particularly careful to avoid the accusation of spamming by following Internet protocols. The company doesn't simply post the entire excerpt to the discussion group site, but instead offers to e-mail the file to those who respond with a request, and it only posts to sites where it is certain people will be interested in the topic.

Functioning much the same as a radio talk show, live chats are now accessed by millions of Internet users. Once the talk is booked, Tenagra writes an introduction for the chat host, creates a list of sample questions, and notifies Web-based chat calendars about the event.

For the Random House children's books mentioned above, Tenagra went a step further. It brought Target stores onboard as a sponsor, and then arranged to set up live chats wherever teachers had access to the Internet in their classrooms. The kids and teachers were thrilled, the authors had a ball, and Random House got tremendous exposure without having to pay any travel expenses.

PUBLIC RELATIONS RESOURCES

In addition to the services of a public relations professional, publishers, authors, and publicity staff can avail themselves of various commercial services:

- Bacon's Information, Inc., 332 South Michigan Avenue, Chicago, IL 60604; Tel. (312) 922-2400 or (800) 621-0561; Fax: (312) 922-3127
  The preeminent public relations resource for media lists, Bacon's publishes print directories and electronic databases of contacts for newspapers, magazines, radio, and television as well as a variety of directories for specific industries and geographic areas. They also provide press-release distribution services.

- Bradley Communications Corp., P.O. Box 1206, Lansdowne, PA 19050-8206; Tel. (800) 784-4359; Fax: (610) 284-3704
  Specializing in serving publishers, Bradley Communications publishes *Radio-TV Interview Report*. This collection of half-page and full-page ads promoting author appearances comes out three times a month and is mailed to radio and television producers. Bradley also offers a comprehensive database of media contacts, which can be purchased in segments on labels, as printed reports, or on disk.

- Burrelle's Information Services, 75 East Northfield Road, Livingston, NJ 07039; Tel. (800) 876-3342
  One of the long-time, leading clipping services, Burrelle's also provides a complete range of media directories in print and CD-ROM formats.

- Business Wire
  Business Wire has twenty-four regional offices. Addresses and phone numbers for these are available online at *www.businesswire.com*. With a primary focus on the business press, this organization can distribute your press release (including photos) online or via fax or e-mail.

- Infocom Group, 5900 Hollis Street, Suite R2, Emeryville, CA 94608-2008; Tel. (800) 959-1059; Fax: (510) 596-9331
  Infocom publishes six different National PR Pitch Books focusing on media contacts in different subject areas. These volumes provide "pitching tips," which offer information on the interests and needs of each media contact. Designed more for public relations professionals and agencies serving a variety of clients, one or more of these books may be helpful for niche publishers.

- PR Wire
  Another commercial press-release distribution service, and the primary competitor to Business Wire, this company offers some interesting selections and has a strong presence in entertainment public relations. They also offer Web site design and maintenance. To find out more or to locate the regional office nearest you, access their Web site at *www.prnewswire.com*.

12

Spectacular Marketing Copy

Though often treated as an after-thought and written by junior marketing staff, the marketing copy—which appears in your press kits, direct-mail promotions, covers, catalogs, and even on your Web site— usually represents your first and perhaps only point of contact with your customers, the media, and the world at large. Effective copy can't sell a book to someone who isn't interested, but it will give you an edge at every point of contact.

Lively, engaging catalog copy can make the difference between a bookstore or library ordering or not ordering a book, and a good press kit will get you more interviews and reviews.

EIGHT RULES FOR EFFECTIVE COPY

While the following rules will apply to a lot of good writing, they are critical elements of most direct mail and most marketing copy. You may quibble that Shakespeare isn't direct, so the rule about simplicity is overstated, or that Hemingway didn't use lists, so the rule on lists is oversimplified. Nevertheless, you will find that most good copy works on the following principles.

CLARITY IS EVERYTHING

You only get one chance with your reader. If your reader has to stop and figure out what you're saying, you've lost him. If your reader hesitates between paragraphs, she isn't going to respond. Every sentence of your copy must be smooth, clean, strong, and persuasive. Every point must anticipate the next point.

Architects don't win awards for designing foundations, but without a well-designed foundation, the building will collapse. Clarity is your foundation. You need to have a clear idea of what you want to accomplish with your piece of writing, even if you don't know how to get there. The process of writing itself can be messy. You may have to throw away ten drafts before you are able to say what you have to say in a simple, direct manner. That's okay. Be as messy as you want, but just don't stop writing until you have said what you need to say with crystal clarity.

BE SPECIFIC

Once you have told your reader how her life will blossom by reading your book, you must follow up that message with real, specific, tangible proof. The poet William Carlos Williams declared, "no ideas but in things." This should be your motto too. Every title among the fifty thousand–plus published yearly offers either to entertain, inform, or inspire. Before readers can choose from among them, however, they need more information. Give them something they can hold on to: scientific data, specifications, any kind of substantive information, a few vivid examples. Even though we agree that statistics lie, we respond to them: "Thirty percent of all headaches strike at 3:00 P.M. on Mondays," or "Book sales are up 15 percent. Are you getting your share of the market?"

MAKE YOUR MESSAGE POSITIVE

Step forward and meet your reader with a positive statement. While this advice seems simple, it's amazing how often publishers violate this rule. Asked by a salesperson to distinguish a new title from the competition, we often fall into explaining how this book is different in negative terms. "It's not like this one. It's not like that one."

Sometimes you just have to go back to the beginning and rephrase the question. "Here's what this book does. It takes the reader by the hand and engages her." Relying on a negative description is like turning your back on the reader.

EMBRACE SIMPLICITY

Sensing that a piece of writing is not doing the job, marketers often pump up their prose, trying to make it cute, fancy, or even profound. However, this usually leads them in the wrong direction. People read a flyer, the back cover of a book, or an advertisement because they're interested in the subject, not because the prose is entertaining. Don't put your writing in their way. Advertising mogul David Ogilvy described how he once got Eleanor Roosevelt to endorse a product. He considered the endorsement a coup, but the ad didn't create sales.

People remembered seeing the former First Lady, but couldn't remember the product she was endorsing. Elaborate prose creates the same problem. The job of marketing copy is to sell books, not itself.

USE THE SECOND PERSON, PRESENT TENSE

In a press release, you don't feature an author who wrote (in the past tense) a book. Your author explains (in the present tense). Her book tells, describes, reveals, shows, helps, explains, thrills, exposes. Your message is current whatever time of day, day of the week, week of the month, or month of the year a person reads your marketing brochure.

Likewise, your flyer can tell your reader that other people have saved their marriages with this book. You'll be more effective, however, by offering them help directly: "Here's how to save your marriage now."

If this looks like a headline on the cover of woman's magazine you might see at the grocery checkout stand, there's a good reason. It's copy that jumps off the page, grabs your attention, and demands an active response.

USE LISTS

Lists work for David Letterman, and they'll work for you. People love lists, whether they provide the structure for books (*Fifty Simple Things*

You Can Do to Save the Earth, Seven Habits of Highly Effective People, The Hundred Best Places to Kiss in Southern California), spiritual systems (the Ten Commandments, the Noble Eightfold Path), or marketing copies. Lists help readers understand what you have to say and they're easy to remember. But, perhaps most important of all, they attract attention.

SELL THE BENEFIT

This is an advertising cliché and the most important of all these rules. People buy books for entertainment, help, information, or inspiration. Using this book you will:

- Double your money by the end of the year
- Lose ten pounds in thirty days
- Get the job you want—today

The benefits are clear: money, weight loss, job. The secret to achieving these ends may be in the book's method, its features, but as consumers or readers, our first interest is the benefit. Similarly, an intricate plot is a feature; a joyful read is a benefit. An intricate plot may make the book a delight to read, but nobody recommends a book just because the plot is intricate.

A further point to keep in mind here is that the benefit may differ depending on your audience. In pitching a radio host on a particular book and author, for instance, all the points described above as benefits are now features. For your media contact, the benefit is a good show, which leads us naturally to the final and most important point.

KNOW YOUR READER

This is not so much a rule as a prerequisite. If you don't know for whom you are writing a piece of copy, take some time to find out. If you are writing direct-mail copy for a professional book, you need to know the concerns of the professionals you are addressing. How will this book meet their needs? What is their test for credibility? What credentials do they look for in an authority? Are they used to purchasing items through the mail? Do they need or respond to a guarantee?

If you can't answer these questions, you may be getting ready to waste a huge amount of money on printing and postage. While different questions may be relevant, the same principle applies to every piece of marketing copy you write—the back cover of a book, a press release, catalog copy, and even your editorial fact sheet. Know who you are writing for, what they need to know, and what will move them to the action you desire. That is your target.

CREATING AN EFFECTIVE PRESS KIT

I've experimented with sending out elaborate press kits, simple press kits, and no press kit—just enclosing a press release with a book. I've sent a simple letter in a business envelope inviting a call for a review copy, and I've tried several other variations on these elements. Since none of these campaigns have been conducted as controlled experiments, I can't say for sure whether one technique is better than the others. I've read articles in which producers and editors have expressed disgust with fancy press kits, and I've heard others say that they like getting all the material these kits offer. From all this, I've concluded that there is no one right package, and so instead of following a formula, I try to create a presentation that's appropriate for the book at hand as well as for the media outlets that I am pitching.

Following is a description of the various pieces that you might send with or without a book.

THE PRESENTATION FOLDER

Much of the glitz and the bulk involved in creating a press kit comes from using a presentation folder, though such a folder is optional. When sending the patent book (described in chapter 10) to technical publications, I chose to keep my presentation to a minimum. I assumed that a folder was not only unnecessary but perhaps even distracting.

In contrast, I consider a nice folder a good investment when sending out to national radio and television shows, and useful as well when I am including a lot of materials, such as backgrounders and sample questions. It's a way to keep materials together, and it gives a professional feel.

While the folder itself can be unadorned, some publishers—seeking brand recognition—will have their company logos printed or embossed on the folders. More commonly, publishers will order over-runs of a book cover and glue the front cover to the front of the port-folio. Displaying the front cover this way acts as a spur and a reminder—hopefully your cover is eye-catching—and it helps your particular kit stand out from the pile on your contact's desk. Having glued the front cover to the portfolio, you can now use the back cover to provide supplementary copy.

THE COVER LETTER

I've seen press kits sent out without cover letters, and I've seen review copies of books sent with only an accompanying press release. I've also noted that it's common practice for publicists to send out generic cover letters with a blanket "Dear Editor/Producer" as a salutation. I suppose that when your time is extremely limited, these practices are necessary and will get by.

If at all possible, however, I suggest sending personalized cover let-ters, something not that difficult once you learn how to use the merge capabilities of your word processor or database. I use the letter to give my best pitch—explaining why this book is important, describing what I consider to be a compelling story suggested by the book, or extolling the author as a great interview subject—and placing myself at my contact's disposal for further information.

My hope in writing this cover letter is that I will increase the response rate among my media contacts and generate a few extra phone calls. Even if this proves wrong, and, of course, I have no way of knowing, I think it's important to put my name as publicist in front of my contact one more time. It means that when I make my follow-up call, there is a better chance that editors or producers will remember me. After all, I remembered them by using their names on my letter.

THE PRESS RELEASE

Written as a news story, the press release answers all the questions your journalism teacher told you to address: Where? What? When? Why? Who? and How? It needs a powerful hook, a catchy headline, and, most important, it must convey the essence of your book. It has to say what is important about this book, how it is different, why someone would want to read it, and whom this book addresses. In addition, it has to be well written, precise, and to the point.

When writing the press release, remember that the book's publication is not itself news unless it is a previously undiscovered manuscript of a deceased Nobel Prize winner. The news is how this book will force a revision of current scientific thinking, or how it will free millions of people from addiction, or how this newly invented guitar method will allow you to play the blues like B. B. King in just three weeks.

While most journalists say that they favor one double-spaced page, I've seen effective two- and three-page press releases. Nevertheless, here's the place to practice the art of concision. Take the time to rewrite and boil down your prose. Two special features that do need to be included in every press release—usually somewhere above the headline—are the release dates and the contact names (with phone numbers). The release date tells journalists the soonest the information in your release should be published. This may be the book's publication date, or, if that date has passed, you can simply indicate "for immediate release." Having the contact name and phone number clearly visible may be the most important element of your press release. This is where producers will look when they want to call you to book an author appearance, request a copy of the book, or simply get more information.

Because book-review editors want the standard specs for a book, ISBN, page count, trim size, format, and price, most book publicists include this information at the bottom of a release.

Supplementary Materials

Depending on who you're pitching and what kind of coverage you're looking for, there's lots more that can be included in your press materials: a single sheet with a short biography, a black-and-white photo of the author, illustrations from the book, a page of favorable testimonial or review quotes, a backgrounder, a tour schedule, suggested interview questions, copies of reviews, and even other articles by the author.

The backgrounder, with extra information that places your book in a context, may be helpful in selling a story to a writer or editor. A book on organizational development, for instance, might have a backgrounder that provides a brief history showing how organizations have evolved. A writer or editor seeing this information might find in it the hook for her own story and decide to proceed.

In contrast, radio talk show hosts may or may not find any value in the backgrounder, but will be glad to find a list of suggested questions. Doing several interviews a day, they may not have more than a few minutes to spend with the book, and so they may use your questions in exactly the form you sent them, or they may also use your questions as a way to get into the subject. I have also heard talk show hosts express disgust with the very idea of receiving suggested questions. As you become personally familiar with media people, you may be able to refine your list and send these pieces only to those who want them.

As noted previously, I don't recommend sending copies of reviews to print sources, but I do send them to radio and television contacts. I have also occasionally included previously published articles by the author as a way to build credibility or to enlarge on a topic. Occasionally, when I have wanted to promote an author as a representative of the publisher, I have also included a profile of the publishing company.

Newspapers will often use a photo of the author to accompany a review, so having a quality black-and-white head shot is important and useful. In addition, print publications will often be glad to make use of a photo or drawing from an attractive, illustrated book. Be sure to include captions with photos.

A final piece for inclusion to television or radio stations is an audiocassette or videotape of an author interview. Though expensive, for the major network television shows, this is a vital element. While most shows don't need this level of reassurance, demonstrating that your author can provide a dynamic program will be a sales point.

SAMPLE PRESS KIT ELEMENTS

Following is a sample press kit provided by my local colleague Patricia Barich and some sample press releases from Maureen Watts, another local colleague.

Created to accompany a galley mailing, the press kit for *Entre-preneurial Couples* (Davies-Black Publishing) by Dr. Kathy Marshack contains a cover letter, press release, biographical sheet, backgrounder, and sample questions. In introducing these pieces, I would like to point out a few features that contribute to their effectiveness.

To begin, notice that the cover letter begins with a hook that suggests the core of a story. The letter introduces the book, but the book itself is a handle for the story. Similarly, the press release features a humorous, suggestive, and entertaining headline. These may seem like frivolous devices, but they tend to be effective. After all, most reporters are seeking dynamic stories, not static books, so if you can point them in the direction of an interesting article—that is, if you can show them how something in the book can be used as the basis for a piece that would be of interest to their readers—you've definitely helped your cause.

I was particularly impressed with the backgrounder for this press kit because it adopts an unusual format by providing important and interesting information through the vehicle of a pair of want ads. More conventional backgrounders might provide sample illustra-tions, supporting information that doesn't appear in the book but would help in the writing of a story, or even a revealing anecdote. In fact, the backgrounder offered here performs the same function as the conventional backgrounder in offering substantive details about the book.

The three press releases that follow each have elements I appre-ciate. I particularly like the headline for the *Stretchware* press release that reads, "The machine that causes the problem now contains the solution." At the same time the copy is tight, clear, and moves along briskly, and there is a nice use of graphic elements.

The *Red Wine for Dummies* press release effectively uses a journey metaphor to turn a conventional guide into something more, while the *Wine for Dummies, Second Edition* release actually makes a story out of the fact that the book has gone to a new edition. This is not a course I would ordinarily recommend, but you can get away with it when the first edition has sold 340,000 copies—a point the press release itself stresses.

PATRICIA BARICH
C O M M U N I C A T I O N S

February 1998

Dear Editor/Producer:

Imagine spending all day every day with your spouse at work. Even in the strongest marriages, some problems would inevitably arise. How do you separate work from home life so that you have some time to relax? What happens when a business disagreement affects your personal relationship or vice versa? How can you be brutally honest with your partner about a professional decision without hurting their feelings? **ENTREPRENEURIAL COUPLES: Making it Work at Work and at Home,** by therapist and business consultant Dr. Kathy Marshack (Davies-Black Publishers, May 1998, hardcover, $26.95, ISBN: 0-89106-115-0) takes on such questions as these, providing the first comprehensive guide on how to work, live and love together successfully.

Geared toward *copreneurs,* couples who start enterprises together; *dual entrepreneurs,* who each have independent ventures; and *solo entrepreneurs with supportive spouses;* **ENTREPRENEURIAL COUPLES** offers readers practical tips on how to improve communication, achieve business and personal goals, be more attentive to their children and find the balance between health and wealth. Marshack blends personal stories from her therapy practice with self-assessment quizzes designed to help anyone better understand their own working style and that of their partner.

A case in point is Marshack's story of husband-and-wife team Stan and Rhonda. Stan decided to invest all his savings and energy into a new business and expected Rhonda to help out in her spare time. But when Rhonda quit her job and tried to work with Stan full-time, he became threatened and possessive of his enterprise. Meanwhile, she felt rejected and didn't understand Stan's motives. With Marshack's guidance, Rhonda realized that she [was] trying to use Stan's business dream as a substitute for her own. After some necessary self-discovery, she found a new job that fulfilled her own ambitions and gave Stan the freedom he needed. Over the years, Marshack has dramatically improved relationships and boosted businesses by helping couples enact this type of simple but critical change.

Kathy Marshack, Ph.D., is a psychotherapist with more than 20 years' experience as a marriage and family therapist and business consultant. With a specialty in consultation to entrepreneurial couples and family-owned businesses, she has a private practice in Vancouver, Washington. She is a columnist on family business issues for the *Vancouver Business Journal* and has been a featured expert on these topics in *Inc.* and *Nation's Business.*

Enclosed please [find] uncorrected galley proofs for **ENTREPRENEURIAL COUPLES** for your review/interview consideration; I will call you soon to determine your interest in Marshack and her book.

Sincerely,

Patsy Barich

870 Market Street · Suite 958 · San Francisco, CA 94102
Phone (415) 433-0551 · Fax (415) 433-0508
E-mail pbarich@pbarich.com

Davies-Black Publishing
A Division of Consulting Psychologists Press, Inc.

415.969.8901
fax 415.988.0673

3803 East Bayshore Road
Palo Alto, California 94303

FOR IMMMEDIATE RELEASE
Contact: Patsy Barich 415/433-0551
Patricia Barich Communications

Should You Sleep With Your Business Partner?

Most people are well aware of the practical wisdom that discourages

employees from indulging in office romance. But what happens when it's the other

way around: when your lifelong mate becomes immersed in your business life,

helping to plan your company's fiscal future along with the evening meal? How do

you separate work from home life so that you have some time to relax? What

happens when a business disagreement affects your personal relationship -- or vice

versa? How can you be brutally honest with your partner about a professional

decision without hurting their feelings?

According to psychotherapist and business consultant Kathy Marshack, Ph.D.,

working with your spouse can be the best or worst thing for building a marriage. In

her new book, **ENTREPRENEURIAL COUPLES: Making it Work at Work and At**

Home, Marshack braves this tricky terrain with more than a few words of wisdom.

Geared toward "copreneurs," couples who start enterprises together; "dual

entrepreneurs," where both members of the couple each have independent

ventures; and "solo entrepreneurs" with supportive spouses; **ENTREPRENEURIAL**

COUPLES offers readers profound insight on and specific direction in how to:

- *improve communication*
- *achieve business and personal goals*
- *be more attentive to their children*
- *find the balance between health and wealth.*

The author blends personal stories from her therapy practice with self-assessment quizzes designed to help readers better understand their own specific working style and that of their partner. Says Marshack, "While most entrepreneurial couples just make do, this book teaches you how to *make the most of your entrepreneurial lifestyle*. . . .[this book] digs into your beliefs and values, where deep, meaningful change really happens." She adds, "You will build a plan to reconstruct your entrepreneurial couple lifestyle in the way that suits you best."

Over the years, Marshack has dramatically improved relationships and boosted businesses by helping couples enact this type of simple but critical change. Unlike many business and career books, Marshack recognizes that there's more to life than making money. By emphasizing private and professional life equally, **ENTREPRENEURIAL COUPLES** offers not only guidance, but a recipe for success.

Kathy Marshack, Ph.D., is a psychotherapist with more than [twenty] years of experience as a marriage and family therapist and business consultant. With a specialty in consultation to entrepreneurial couples and family-owned businesses, she has a private practice in Vancouver, Wash. She is a columnist on family business issues for the *Vancouver Business Journal* and has been a featured expert on these topic[s] in *Inc.* magazine and *Nation's Business*.

ENTREPRENEURIAL COUPLES: Making It Work at Work and at Home
by Kathy Marshack
Davies-Black Publishing, May 1998
$26.95, hardcover, 264 pages
ISBN: 0-89106-115-0

Please send us two copies of your review.

Contact: Patsy Barich 415/433-0551
Patricia Barich Communications
e-mail: pbarich@pbarich.com

Kathy Marshack, Ph.D , author of
ENTREPRENEURIAL COUPLES: Making It Work at Work and at Home

Kathy Marshack is a psychologist in private practice whose specialty lies in consultation to family-owned businesses. With more than 20 years of experience as a marriage and family therapist and a business consultant, she has been profiled in *Inc.*, *Nation's Business*, and the Wells Fargo Bank magazine *Business '97* for her professional expertise. She is a member of the National Association of Social Workers and the American Psychological Association, and she is a board certified diplomate in social work.

Marshack received her B.S. degree (1972) in psychology from Portland State University, her M.S.W. degree (1975) from the University of Hawaii, and her Ph.D. degree (1994) in psychology from the Fielding Institute. She has presented her research at local, national, and international conferences. A regular columnist for the *Vancouver Business Journal*, she has contributed numerous articles to newspapers and journals on topics relevant to families in business.

ENTREPRENEURIAL COUPLES is more than just a professional endeavor: it reflects Marshack's personal life as well as she works to balance her roles as an entrepreneur, a dual-career wife, and a team parent. Marshack lives in Vancouver, Wash., with her husband, Howard, a family law attorney, and their two daughters, Bianca and Phoebe.

Desperately Seeking Sanity:
How to keep your business from ruining your marriage (and vice versa)

Kathy Marshack, Ph.D., author of **ENTREPRENEURIAL COUPLES: Making It Work at Work and at Home**, presents two tongue-in-cheek personal ads that show how unrealistic expectations can make for some very real business and marital problems:

MAN SEEKING WIFE/BUSINESS PARTNER

Successful businessman seeks life partner to share my entrepreneurial dream. Must believe in me and be supportive of the long hours required of a start-up venture. Nothing is too much for you in that you are comfortable juggling the many demands of the wife of an entrepreneur. . . household, childcare, social obligations and working late hours at the office to meet deadlines. Opportunity to develop your own very satisfying career as you help me build my business. Your rewards are financial security, the opportunity to be part of something big, and the chance to work side-by-side with your husband. At work you are my hard-working right hand person. At home you are the loving support that makes the long hours worthwhile.

WOMAN SEEKING HUSBAND/BUSINESS PARTNER

Career-minded, college-educated woman with entrepreneurial spirit, tired of facing the "glass ceiling" of corporate life, seeks like-minded college-educated male to share love and business partnership in a start-up venture. Must believe in egalitarian relationships, sharing fully in the household maintenance as well as sharing equally in the ownership, management and responsibility of our joint business venture. Even though you possess creativity and leadership skills which you use to help me create the "American Dream," your ego is not bruised by my ability to make decisions and take charge. At work, you are dedicated, aggressive and single-minded in your pursuit of success for our business. At home you relax and become playful because you are a loving, sensitive, communicative male, who adores me and takes the time to get to know our children.

Do these profiles sound too good to be true? That's because they are, explains Kathy Marshack, whose book shows readers how to put aside romantic fantasies, and build strong family businesses on hard work and honest communication.

Contact: Patsy Barich 415/433-0551
Patricia Barich Communications

Contact: Patsy Barich 415/433-0551
Patricia Barich Communications

**Questions for Kathy Marshack, Ph.D., author of
ENTREPRENEURIAL COUPLES:**

1. What are the right reasons to go into business with your spouse? What are the wrong ones?

2. Are there some couples whom you advise not to work together? If so, how do you identify them?

3. In your book, you identify three types of entrepreneurial couples: "copreneurs," "dual entrepreneurs" and "solo entrepreneurs with supportive spouses." Which of these three tends to work out the most smoothly? Which has the most potential for conflict?

4. What are a few simple ways that couples in business can improve communication?

5. Do you find that gender affects how people conduct business? Are men and women instinctively inclined toward different patterns?

6. How has your own experience as an entrepreneur affected your theories on the subject? What have you and your family learned through the years?

7. How can couples learn to put away business concerns and enjoy time together at home?

8. How does being part of an entrepreneurial couple affect your ability to parent effectively? What are the common parenting pitfalls to watch out for?

9. Can business failure become an opportunity for strengthening a marriage?

10. In **ENTREPRENEURIAL COUPLES**, you argue against compromising too much of yourself in business. How can two distinct individuals retain their unique goals without butting heads?

11. You write that the couple bond is a key ingredient for business success. What happens when a marriage between two business partners disintegrates? Can the business be saved?

12. In your book, you draw on your years as a therapist and use several real life examples of couples in business. Which of these best epitomizes a healthy "entrepreneurial couple"?

Shelter Publications, Inc.

For Immediate Release

Contact: Maureen Watts
Publicist (415) 826-9488
email: maureen@stretchware.com

The machine that causes the problem now contains the solution!

STRETCH*WARE*™
THE SOFTWARE THAT REMINDS YOU
TO **S T R E T C H !**

Back pain, stiff muscles, tight joints, tension, and stress. Every day millions of Americans feel the aches and pains brought on by long hours sitting at a desk and using a computer. Repetitive strain injuries have risen 80% since 1990, according to the U.S. Bureau of Labor Statistics. And while ergonomics are essential in the workplace, our bodies still suffer from long periods of sitting and inactivity.

To address the growing problem of workplace injuries, experts have recommended taking breaks and stretching—a simple activity that can make you feel better. However, most people will not make the time to take a stretching break—they need to be reminded.

StretchWare™, by stretching expert Bob Anderson, author of *Stretching* and *Stretching at Your Computer or Desk*, is the computer software that reminds you to stretch. **StretchWare**™ can be tailored to meet each individual's work situation and personal requirements. You choose three methods of activating the reminder: at regular intervals (for example, every 45 minutes, or one hour); at specific times of the day (such as 10:30, 11:45); or by number of keystrokes/mouseclicks.

To get your attention, you choose a sound (Tibetan bell, harp, or clock), a flashing icon to appear in the taskbar, and/or a pop-up window asking if you have time to stretch. If you click "yes," the stretches come onto your screen.

StretchWare™ is easy to use. Installation takes just a few minutes. Set your preferences and you are ready to stretch! There are 14 different stretching routines, including:

- Good Morning! Startup Stretches
- Lower Back Stretches
- On-the-Phone Stretches
- Keyboard Operator Stretches
- Online Stretches
- Stressed-Out Stretches

Each routine has six stretches and takes a total of one to two minutes to complete. Instructions for doing each stretch pop up when you roll your mouse over that stretch. Check out Shelter Publications' website at http://www.stretchware.com to try a free, 30-day demo of **StretchWare**™.

StretchWare™—**The Software That Reminds You To Stretch!**
 by Bob Anderson
 Version 1.0, for Macintosh and Windows 95, 98, or NT

Contact: Maureen Watts
Phone (415) 826-9488
Fax (415) 826-6355
Email: wattsmo@earthlink.net

For Review Copies call:
Catherine Schmitz/IDG Books
(415) 655-3027

RED WINE FOR DUMMIES ™

Authors of the popular bestseller, *WINE FOR DUMMIES,*™
solve the mysteries of red wine

Foster City, California, October 17, 1996 — Do you love red wine but admittedly have only tried Cabernet Sauvignon? Are you a seasoned red wine oenophile, but would like a handy reference guide filled with notes on many of the world's wine producers and vineyards, a red wine vintage chart, and a thousand red wine recommendations—without tedious tasting notes? In either case, *Red Wine For Dummies* is the book for you.

Written by wine experts Mary Ewing-Mulligan and Ed McCarthy—the authors of the runaway bestseller, *Wine For Dummies*—this book is a tour de force of the highly complicated and deliciously rich world of red wine. *Red Wine For Dummies* breaks through the layers of intimidation and complexity of red wine with a highly accessible yet comprehensive teaching approach.

The authors begin with the basics—explanations of the different kinds of grapes and types of red wine—and then embark readers on an armchair tour and wine "tasting" through the world's many wine regions. Readers discover a red wine universe of aromas and flavors ranging from earthy to oaky, stemmy to herbal, vegetal to leather, barnyard to berry.

Starting out on the West Coast, we learn about California Cabernet Sauvignon and Merlot—the state's most popular grapes and wine. A discussion of Pinot Noir crosses the California border into Oregon, followed by a perusal of Washington state's world-class Merlots. A journey to the East Coast reveals Long Island, New York's thriving wine country, where some of the most successful wines are blends of Merlot, Cabernet Sauvignon, Cabernet Franc, and Petite Verdot. Next, the authors take us "down under" to discover the famously distinct red wines of Australia,

DUMMIES INC.
IDG BOOKS WORLDWIDE, INC.
919 E. Hillsdale Blvd., Suite 400 Foster City, CA 94404 **TEL** 650.655.3000 **FAX** 650.655.3299

w w w . d u m m i e s . c o m

Chile, Argentina, and South Africa. Finally, we venture overseas again to the very roots of winemaking in Europe. Through tours of the vineyards of France, Italy, and Spain readers become well acquainted with the seven classic types of red wine: Burgundy, Bordeaux, Beaujolais, Chianti, Rioja, Côte Rôtie and Hermitage.

Throughout, *Red Wine For Dummies* provides the authors' choices for specific red wines and vintages. In addition, the book offers tips on pairing red wine with food, and challenges readers with ten hands-on wine-tasting exercises for sharpening their palates. A glossary of red wine terms and a crucial pronunciation guide are also included, as well as contact information for wineries whose wines are available only through the mail.

With *Red Wine For Dummies*, wine lovers have a treasure trove of practical advice to the bountiful world of red wine in a down-to-earth, witty, and handy little book packed with information.

"Having these books in your pocket is the next best thing to taking these two wine authorities to the retail store with you."
—*Wine & Spirits* 1997 Buying Guide

"*White Wine For Dummies* and *Red Wine For Dummies* are something close to miraculous in their combination of readability, expertise and plain common sense."
—*New York Daily News*

ABOUT THE AUTHORS

Mary Ewing-Mulligan, Master of Wine is co-owner and director of the International Wine Center in New York. In 1994 she was named Wine Educator of the Year by Wine America, an annual trade show. She is the only American woman who is a Master of Wine, signifying the highest level of knowledge in the wine industry.

Ed McCarthy is a wine collector, writer, instructor, and consultant who has been active in the wine trade for 20 years. He contributes to *Wine Enthusiast* magazine and is an editor of the *Underground Wine Journal*. The two authors are married and live in Long Island, New York.

About IDG Books Worldwide, Inc.

IDG Books Worldwide, Inc., is headquartered in Foster City, CA, and is an International Data Group Company. IDG Books Worldwide publishes the bestselling ...For Dummies series, with over 30 million books currently in print in 30 languages around the world. There are over 230 ...For Dummies titles which cover software, hardware, the Internet, business, hobbies, and personal development topics. See http://www.dummies.com. ...For Dummies and the Dummies Man are registered trademarks under exclusive license to IDG Books Worldwide, Inc., from International Data Group, Inc.

Contact: Maureen Watts, Publicist
(415) 826-9488

Three hundred and forty thousand wine lovers can't be wrong!

Wine For Dummies,® 2nd Edition
A complete update of the beloved bestselling book on wine

(Foster City, California, October, 1998)—*Wine For Dummies*, the award-winning, entertaining, and unpretentious guide to wine that became one of IDG Books Worldwide's bestselling non-computer books, has been completely updated by renowned authors and wine experts Ed McCarthy and Mary Ewing-Mulligan.

Wine For Dummies, 2nd Edition provides readers with a new and expanded version of what has been called the "wine lover's bible." Favored by both wine novices and connoisseurs for its accessible teaching style and fun approach to the complex world of wine, *Wine For Dummies* has become <u>the</u> recommended book on wine. Winning the Georges Duboeuf Wine Book of the Year Award in 1995, critics have called *Wine For Dummies* "the grand cru of wine books," and "a delightfully formatted compendium of everything you need to know about wine." The runaway bestseller has over 340,000 copies in print, has gone back to press eleven times, and has been translated into twelve languages.

Why a new edition? "Wine is a living, dynamic substance. New vintages and wines appear each year, and new wineries open up, while others close down," explain McCarthy and Ewing-Mulligan. Based on readers' responses from the first edition, *Wine For Dummies, 2nd Edition* now includes:

- A newly restructured and better organized text

- Highlights of new wineries, current wine prices, and new bargains

- The scoop on new vintages—including an updated vintage chart

- Two brand new appendixes: a pronunciation guide to major wine terms and a wine glossary

- Entire chapters devoted to the wine regions of Italy and the USA

DUMMIES INC.
IDG BOOKS WORLDWIDE, INC.
919 E. Hillsdale Blvd., Suite 400 Foster City, CA 94404 **TEL** 650.655.3000 **FAX** 650.655.3299

w w w . d u m m i e s . c o m

Wine For Dummies, 2nd Edition is brimming with all the authoritative information on wine that the first edition had, including how to:

- ✓ **Open and pour wine properly**
- ✓ **Taste wine**
- ✓ **Recognize good wine from bad wine**
- ✓ **Read wine labels**
- ✓ **Speak the language of wine**
- ✓ **Navigate restaurant wine lists**
- ✓ **Select and buy wine**

With the holidays approaching, readers shouldn't miss chapter 20, "Marrying Wine With Food," and Chapter 15 "Bubbling Beauties," on the mysteries and delights of Champagne and other bubblies. Wine connoisseurs will be interested in Part Four "When You've Caught the Bug," including sections on wine buying and collecting, recommended publications for further reading, and special wine sites on the internet.

In short, *Wine For Dummies, 2nd Edition* offers wine lovers of every level a completely up-to-date reference book, wine textbook, and user's manual, all in one. The book is the perfect gift for fans of the first edition, those who may want to buy a new edition as a gift, as well as anyone looking for a definitive source of information on wine.

<u>About the Authors</u>
Mary Ewing-Mulligan is the director of the International Wine Center in New York. She is one of 224 Masters of Wine in the world and the only female Master of Wine in the United States. Ed McCarthy is a certified wine educator, writer, collector, and consultant who's been active in the wine trade for over 20 years. McCarthy is a regular contributor to *Wine Enthusiast* magazine and *The Wine Journal*. Together, the husband and wife writing team have written the popular books *Red Wine For Dummies*®(1996), *White Wine For Dummies*®(1996), and *Wine Buying Companion For Dummies*®(1997).

<u>About IDG Books, Worldwide</u>
IDG Books Worldwide, Inc., headquartered in Foster City, CA, is a leading publisher of technology, business and self-help books, including the best-selling *...For Dummies*®, *...Secrets*®, and *Teach Yourself* ® series. IDG Books Worldwide has more than 700 active titles plus books translated into 36 languages around the world.

More information about IDG Books Worldwide is available from the company's SEC filings (NASDAQ: IDGB) or by visiting its Web sites: www.idgbooks.com or www.dummies.com. IDG Books Worldwide is a subsidiary of International Data Group, Inc., a leading global provider of information technology media, research, conferences and expositions.

...For Dummies is a registered trademark, and Dummies Man is a trademark of IDG Books Worldwide, Inc.

Wine For Dummies,® *2nd Edition*
Ed McCarthy and Mary Ewing-Mulligan
Price: $19.99, Pages: 430, 7 3/8 x 9 1/4 inches paperback
ISBN 0-7645-5114-0
Publication date: October 1998

Concluding Thoughts

Although it sounds a little like a parody of Newton, I have found that the process of marketing consumes as much energy as it is given. Whether you're a publisher or an author, whether you're promoting one book or a huge list, there's always more that can be done. Since we all work within certain limitations—time, energy, resources, vision, and so on—it's important to monitor the results of our efforts and to know when to move on.

How do you know when? Hopefully, the preceding chapters have made it clear that there isn't a simple answer to this question. My favorite answer is to say that if you are doing things right, then even in moving on you will be extending and supporting your previous efforts—your career as a writer, your publishing company, your relationships with your target audience, your own understanding of how to market successfully.

Beyond the reassurance that in a perfect universe no effort goes to waste, I would also like to add that having mastered the challenges of the last book or the last season's list, we immediately find that we need new skills and new insights for our current projects. In the words of

T. S. Eliot, "one has only learnt to get the better of words/For the thing one no longer has to say." Even as I put the finishing touches on this book, I am accumulating material for the next edition—a file of articles, thoughts, notes, and observations.

Not surprisingly, as I look in this file, I find that the bulk of the material relates to electronic publishing. That's the cutting edge. That's what's new and changing, and there is no doubt in my mind that these changes will affect all of the ways in which publishing is done. Not that books will disappear—movies didn't kill books, TV didn't kill books, and computers didn't kill books. Nevertheless, the digital age is affecting the role of books, the look of books, the way books are used, and the way books are marketed. It will probably also affect and limit the kinds of materials that are ultimately produced in the traditional printed and bound format that we call a book. The foreseeable future contains books, but it also holds the promise of a lot of other ways for providing the kinds of things we are accustomed to getting from books.

As noted earlier, publishers and readers have already found that certain kinds of reference material is better suited to delivery on CDs than printed and bound. Are they still books? Does it matter? It doesn't—unless your job as a publisher or author is to produce something that looks and feels like the book you have always known and loved. While moving from one form of delivery to another may be a small stretch, I think it will prove only a warm-up exercise for the changes to come. And, although I have spent my life treasuring books and the paper they are printed on, I am excited about these new developments as a reader, writer, and publishing professional. My optimism rests on two assumptions. One, that in the future people will have the same need that they have ever had to communicate thoughts, feelings, and information to one another and, perhaps, even more so. In other words, that the words, images, and creative spirit found in books today will continue to be produced in some form or other. And two, that people will have to continue working hard to find each other in order to consummate this act of communication, so that marketing will always be a value-added function of publishing.

Resources

BOOKS

Appelbaum, Judith. *How to Get Happily Published*. New York: HarperCollins, 1998.

Balkin, Richard. *A Writer's Guide to Contract Negotiations*. Cincinnati, OH: Writer's Digest Books, 1985.

Blanco, Jodee. *The Complete Guide to Book Publicity*. New York: Allworth Press, 2000.

Bly, Robert W. *The Copywriter's Handbook*. New York: Henry Holt, 1990.

Bunnin, Brad and Peter Beren. *The Writer's Legal Companion*. Reading, MA: Perseus Books, 1998.

Crawford, Tad. *Business and Legal Forms for Authors and Self-Publishers*. New York: Allworth Press, 1996.

Crawford, Tad and Tony Lyons. *The Writer's Legal Guide*. New York: Allworth Press, 1996.

Holm, Kristen C., editor. *Writer's Market*. Cincinnati, OH: Writer's Digest. Annual.

Huenefeld, John. *The Huenefeld Guide to Book Publishing*. Bedford, MA: Mills and Sanderson, 1990.

International Literary Market Place. New Providence, NJ: R. R. Bowker. Annual.

Kirsch, Jonathan. *Kirsch's Handbook of Publishing Law*. Venice, CA: Acrobat Books, 1995.

Kremer, John. *1001 Ways to Market Your Books*. Fairfield, IA: Open Horizons, 1998.

Larsen, Michael. *How to Write a Book Proposal*. Cincinnati, OH: Writer's Digest, 1997.

Larsen, Michael. *Literary Agents*. New York: John Wiley and Sons, Inc., 1996.

Literary Market Place. New Providence, NJ: R. R. Bowker. Annual.

Mathiesen, Michael. *Marketing on the Internet*. Gulf Breeze, FL: Maximum Press, 1997.

Mettee, Stephen Blake. *How to Write a Nonfiction Book Proposal*. Fresno, CA: Quill Driver Books, 2002.

Mutchler, John C., ed. *The American Directory of Writer's Guidelines*. Fresno, CA: Quill Driver Books, 1997.

Nash, Edward L. *Direct Marketing: Strategy, Planning, Execution*. New York: McGraw-Hill, 1994.

Ogilvy, David. *Ogilvy on Advertising*. New York: Random House, 1987.

Page, Susan. *The Shortest Distance Between You and a Published Book*. New York: Broadway Books, 1997.

Shiva, V.A. *The Internet Publicity Guide*. New York: Allworth Press, 1997.

Stone, Bob. *Successful Direct Marketing Methods*. Lincolnwood, IL: NTC Business Books, 1988.

Van Yoder, Steven. *Get Slightly Famous*. Berkeley, CA: Bay Tree Publishing, 2003.

Woll, Thomas. *Publishing for Profit*. Tucson, AZ.: Fisher Books, 1998.

MAGAZINES AND NEWSLETTERS

Book Marketing Update. Bradley Communications Corp., 135 East Plumstead Avenue, Lansdowne, PA 19050; Tel. (800) 989-1400.

Book Publishing Report. Cowles Simba Information, 11 Riverbend Drive S., Stamford, CT 06907; Tel. (800) 307-2529; Web site: *www.simbanet.com*.

Booklist. American Library Association, 50 E. Huron Street, Chicago, IL 60611; Tel. (312) 944-6780.

Bulldog Reporter's Book Marketing and Publicity. Infocom Group, 5900 Hollis Street, Suite R2, Emeryville, CA 94608; Tel. (800) 959-1059.

Feminist Bookstore News. P.O. Box 882554, San Francisco, CA 94188; Tel. (415) 626-1556.

Folio. Cowles Business Media, 11 Riverbend Drive S., Stamford, CT 06907; Tel. (800) 307-2529; Web site: *www.mediacentral.com/Market/SourceBook/*.

Horn Book. 11 Beacon Street, Suite 1000, Boston, MA 02108; Tel. (800) 325-1170.

Independent Publisher. Jenkins Group, 121 E. Front Street, Third Floor, Traverse City, MI 49684; Tel. (616) 933-0445; Web site: *www.bookpublishing.com.*

Kirkus Reviews. 200 Park Avenue S., New York, NY 10003; Tel. (212) 777-4554.

Library Journal. Cahners Publishing Co., 245 W. 17th Street, New York, NY 10010; Tel. (212) 463-6819; Web site: *www.ljdigital.com.*

Publishers Weekly. Cahners Publishing Co., 245 W. 17th Street, New York, NY 10010; Tel. (212) 463-6758.

RQ. American Library Association, 50 E. Huron Street, Chicago, IL, 60611; Tel. (312) 944-6780.

School Library Journal. Cahners Publishing Co., 245 W. 17th Street, New York, NY 10010; Tel. (212) 463-6759.

ONLINE RESOURCES

Bookselling This Week (*http://news.bookweb.org*)

Booksense (*http://news.bookweb.org/booksense*)

Children's Educational Cooperative (*www.childrens-educational-coop.com*)

Pub-Forum (*owner-pub-forum@majordomo.alentus.com*)

PublishersLunch (*publisherslunch@topica.email-publisher.com*)

PW NewsLine (*http://publishersweekly.reviewsnews.com/subscribe.asp*)

PUBLISHING INDUSTRY
AND AUTHOR ORGANIZATIONS

American Book Producers Association, 156 Fifth Ave., New York, NY 10010; phone (800) 209-4575; e-mail: *office@abpaonline.org*; *www.abpaonline.org*.

American Booksellers Association, 828 S. Broadway, Tarrytown, NY 10591; phone (800) 637-0037; e-mail: *info@bookweb.org*; *www.bookweb.org*.

American Institute of Graphic Arts, 164 Fifth Ave., New York, NY 10010; phone (212) 807-1990; e-mail: *comments@aiga.org*; *www.aiga.org*.

American Library Association, 50 E. Huron St., Chicago, IL 60611; phone (312) 944-6780; e-mail: *webmaster@ala.org*; *www.ala.org*.

American Society of Journalists and Authors, 1501 Broadway, Suite 302, New York, NY 10036; phone (212) 768-7414; e-mail: *execdir@asja.org*; *www.asja.org*.

American Wholesale Booksellers Association, 702 S. Michigan St., South Bend, IN 46601; phone (219) 232-8500; e-mail: *info@thedistributors.com*; *www.thedistributors.com*.

Antiquarian Booksellers' Association of America, 20 W. 44th St., 4th floor, New York, NY 10036-6604; phone (212) 944-8291; e-mail: *inquiries@abaa.org*; *www.abaa.org*.

Arizona Book Publishing Association, 957 E. Guadalupe Rd., Box 20, Tempe, AZ 85283; phone (602) 274-6264; e-mail: *info@azbookpub.com*; *www.azbookpub.com*.

Association of American Publishers, 71 Fifth Ave., 2nd floor, New York, NY 10003-3004; phone (212) 255-0200; e-mail: *amyg@publishers.org*; *www.publishers.org*.

Association of American University Presses, Inc., 71 West 23rd St., New York, NY 10010; phone (212) 989-1010; e-mail: *webmaster@aaupnet.org*; *www.aaupnet.org*.

Association of Authors and Publishers, 6124 Hwy., 6 North, PMB 109, Houston, TX 77084; phone (281) 340-0185; e-mail: *info@authorsandpublishers.org*; *www.authorsandpublishers.org*.

The Authors Guild, Inc., 31 E. 28th St., 10th floor, New York, NY 10016-7923; phone (212) 563-5904; e-mail: *staff@authorsguild.org*; *www.authorsguild.org*.

Bay Area Independent Publishers Association, P.O. Box E, Corte Madera, CA 94976; phone (415) 430-2196, ext. 1175; e-mail: *baipa@onebox.com*; *www.baipa.net*.

Black Writers Alliance, Inc., P.O. Box 700065, Dallas, TX 75370; phone (214) 722-1100; e-mail: *info@blackwriters.org*; *www.black-writers.org*.

Book Industry Study Group, 19 W. 21st St., Suite 905, New York, NY 10010; phone (646) 336-7141; e-mail: *bisg-info@bisg.org*; *www.bisg.org*.

Book Manufacturer's Institute, Inc., 65 William St., Suite 300, Wellesley, MA 02181-4007; phone (781) 239-0103; e-mail: *info@bmibook.com*; *www.bmibook.com*.

Book Publishers Northwest, 350 N. 74th St., Seattle, WA; phone (206) 322-6442; e-mail: *bpnwnews@aol.com*.

Book Publishers of Texas, 6387-B Camp Bowie #340, Fort Worth, TX 76116; phone (817) 247-6016; e-mail: *bookpublishersoftexas@worldnet.att.net*; *www.bookpublishersoftexas.com*.

Catholic Book Publishers Association, 8404 Jamesport Drive, Rockford, IL 61108; e-mail: *cbpa3@aol.com*; *www.cbpa.org*.

Carolina Association of Publishers, c/o John Simone, Three Pyramids Publishing, 201 Kenwood Meadows Dr., Raleigh, NC 27603-8314; phone: (919) 773-2080; e-mail: *JFS999@mindspring.com*.

The Children's Book Council, 12 W. 37th St., 2nd floor, New York, NY 10018-7480; phone (212) 966-1990; e-mail: *info@cbcbooks.org*; *www.cbcbooks.org*.

Children's Educational Cooperative, P.O. Box 23565, Columbia, SC 29224; phone (803) 736-9797; e-mail info@playandteach.com; *www.playandteach.com*.

Christian Booksellers Association, Inc., P.O. Box 62000, Colorado Springs, CO 80901; phone (800) 252-1950; e-mail: *info@cbaonline.org*; *www.cbaonline.org*.

Colorado Independent Publishers Association, P.O. Box 861, Broomfield, CO 80038-0861; phone (303) 436-1982; e-mail: *info@cipabooks.com*; *www.cipabooks.com*.

Connecticut Authors and Publishers Association, Attn: Brian Jud, P.O. Box 715, Avon, CT 06001-0715; phone (800) 562-4357; e-mail: *capa@strongbooks.com*; *www.aboutcapa.com*.

Consortium of Northern Publishers, P.O. Box 60529, Fairbanks, AK 99706-0529; phone (907) 474-4969.

The Feminist Bookstore Network, P.O. Box 882554, San Francisco, CA 94188; phone (415) 642-9993; e-mail: *fbn@fembknews.com*; *www.litwomen.org/wip/stores.html*.

Florida Publishers Association, Inc., P.O. Box 430, Highland City, FL 33846-0430; phone (863) 648-4420; e-mail: *FPAbooks@aol.com*; *www.flbookpub.org*

The Greater New York Independent Publishers Association, c/o Small Press Center, 20 W. 44th St., New York, NY 10036; phone (212) 764-7021; e-mail: *info@smallpress.org*; *www.smallpress.org/articles/gnyipa.htm*.

Hawaii Book Publishers Association, P.O. Box 235736, Honolulu, HI 96823-3512; phone (808) 734-7159; e-mail: *aloha@hawaiibooks.org*; *www.hawaiibooks.org*.

Illinois Woman's Press Association, P.O. Box 59256, Schaumburg, IL 60159; phone (312) 458-9151; *www.iwpa.com*.

Independent Publishers of New England, c/o Shel Horowitz, P.O. Box 1164, Northampton, MA 01061; phone (413) 586-2388; e-mail: *Publishers@IPNEonline.com*; *www.IPNEonline.com*.

Independent Publishers Association of Canada, Box 22184, Bankers Hall, Calgary, Alberta T2P 4J1 Canada; phone (403) 234-8565; e-mail: *info@ipac-publishers.com*; *www.ipac-publishers.com*.

MidAtlantic Publishers Association, c/o Bookwise Associates, P.O. Box 50277, Baltimore, MD 21211; phone (410) 261-5593; e-mail: *info@midatlanticpublishers.org*; *www.midatlanticpublishers.org*.

Midwest Independent Publishers Association, P.O. Box 581432, Minneapolis, MN 55458-1432; phone (651) 917-0021; e-mail: *info@mipa.org*; *www.mipa.org*.

Minnesota Book Publishers Roundtable, c/o Brad Vogt, 40214 Wallaby Road, Rice, MN 56367; phone (320) 249-9806; *bvogt@cloudnet.com*; *www.publishersroundtable.org*.

Multicultural Publishing and Education Catalog, 177 South Kihei Rd., Maui, HI 96753; phone (808) 984-1440; e-mail: *editors@gamekids.com*; *www.mpec.org*.

National Association of College Stores, Inc., 500 E. Lorain St., Oberlin, OH 44074-1298; (800) 622-7498; e-mail: *webteam@nacs.org*; *www.nacs.org*.

National Association of Wholesaler-Distributors, 1725 K St. NW, Suite 300, Washington, DC 20006-1419; phone (202) 872-0885; e-mail: *naw@nawd.org*; *www.naw.org*.

National Association of Women Writers, P.O. Box 183812, Arlington, TX 76096; phone (866) 821-5829; e-mail: *naww@onebox.com*; *www.naww.org*.

National Book Foundation, 95 Madison Ave., Suite 709, New York, NY 10016; phone (212) 685-0261; e-mail: *natbkfdn@ mindspring.com*; *www.nationalbook.org*.

National Writers Association, 3140 S. Peoria, #295, Aurora, CO 80014; phone (303) 841-0246; e-mail: *execdir@nationalwriters. com*; *www.nationalwriters.com*.

Network of Alternatives, Publishers, Retailers and Artists, P.O. Box 9, 109 North Beach, Eastsound, WA 98245; phone (360) 376-2702; e-mail: *napraexec@napra.com*; *www.napra.com*.

New Age Publishers and Retailing Alliance—See Network of Alternatives, Publishers, Retailers and Artists.

New Mexico Book Association, P.O. Box 1285, Santa Fe, NM 87504; phone (505) 983-1412; e-mail: *oceantree@earthlink.net*; *www.nmbook.org*.

Northwest Association of Book Publishers, P.O. Box 3786, Wilsonville, OR 97070-3786; phone (503) 223-9055; e-mail: *info@nwabp.org*; *www.nwabp.org*.

Organization of Book Publishers of Ontario, 720 Bathurst St., Suite 301, Toronto, Ontario M5S 2R4, Canada; phone (416) 536-7692; e-mail: *obpo@interlog.com*; *www.ontariobooks.ca*.

Periodical and Book Association of America, Inc., 481 Eighth Ave., Suite 803, New York, NY 10001; phone (212) 689-4952; e-mail: *info@pbaa.net*; *www.pbaa.net*.

Publishers Association of the South, 4412 Fletcher St., Panama City, FL 32405; phone (850) 914-0766; e-mail: *executive@pubsouth.org*; *www.pubsouth.org*.

Publishers and Writers of San Diego, c/o Robert Goodman (Silvercat), 3738 Carmel View Rd., San Diego, CA 92130; phone (858) 794-1597; e-mail: *pwsd@silvercat.com*; *www.publishersandwriters.org*.

Publishers Marketing Association, 627 Aviation Way, Manhattan Beach, CA 90266; phone (310) 372-2732; e-mail: *info@pma-online.org*; *www.pma-online.org*.

The Reference Society, 21 Greenhouse Lane, Poughkeepsie, NY 12601; phone (845) 473-3719; e-mail: *directorieswiz@aol.com*; *www.d-net.com/refsoc*

Sacramento Publishers and Authors Association, P.O. Box 161053, Sacramento, CA 95816; phone (916) 444-0117; e-mail: *info@sacpublishers.org*; *www.sacpublishers.org* or *www.sacauthors.org*.

San Diego Publishers Alliance—*See* Publishers and Writers of San Diego.

Small Publishers, Artists and Writers Network, PMB 123, 323 E. Matilija St., Suite 110, Ojai, CA 93023; phone (818) 886-4281; e-mail: *info@spawn.org*; *www.spawn.org*.

Small Publishers Association of North America, P.O. Box 1306, 425 Cedar St., Buena Vista, CO 81211; phone (719) 395-4790; e-mail: *span@spannet.org*; *www.spannet.org*.

St. Louis Publishers Association, P.O. Box 700, Eureka, MO 63025; phone (636) 938-3348; e-mail: *SLPA@staircasepress.com*; *www.stlouispublishers.org*.

Southern Independent Publishers, 12610 Hwy. 90 West, Grand Bay, AL 36541; phone (334) 865-1500; e-mail: *boellis25@aol.com*; *www.laughingowl.com/sips.htm*.

Upper Peninsula Publishers and Authors Association, Attn: Moira Wilson (President), P.O. Box 484, Hessel, MI 49745; phone (906) 484-2708; e-mail: *moirazw@cedarville.net*; *www.manytracks.com/uppaa*.

REGIONAL BOOKSELLERS ASSOCIATIONS

Canadian Booksellers Association, 789 Don Mills Rd., #700, Toronto, Ontario M3C 1T5 Canada; phone (866) 788-0790; e-mail: *sdayus@cbabook.org*; *www.cbabook.org*.

Chesapeake Regional Area Booksellers, c/o Michael Sullivan (President), Reprint Book Shop, 455 L'Enfant Plaza SW, Washington, DC 20024-2192; phone (202) 554-5070.

Gateway Booksellers Association, Gus Churchill, 12750 Coachlight Square Dr., Florissant, MO 63033.

Great Lakes Booksellers Association, Jim Dana (Executive Director), P.O. Box 901, 208 Franklin St., Grand Haven, MI 49417; phone (800) 745-2460; e-mail: *glba@books-glba.org*; *www.books-glba.org*.

Houston Area Booksellers Association, Linda Branick (President), c/o Booktronics, 3370 Westheimer Ave., Houston, TX 77056; phone (713) 626-4000.

Intermountain Booksellers Association, Danni Davis (President), c/o Signature Books, 564 West 400 North, Salt Lake City, UT 84116; phone (801) 484-9100.

Intermountain Booksellers Association, P.O. Box 56, Riverton, UT 84065; phone (801) 254-1933.

Mid-South Independent Booksellers Association, Andy Jackson (Executive Director), 15911 Whispering Falls Ct., Houston, TX 77084-2913; phone (281) 656-2130; e-mail: *andy@msiba.org*; *www.msiba.org*.

Midwest Booksellers Association, Ellen Scott (President), c/o The Bookhouse, 3808 South 109th St., Omaha, NE 68144; phone (402) 392-1931; e-mail: *EWSbooks@aol.com*.

Minnesota Book Publishers Roundtable, c/o Tricia Theurer, Voyageur Press, 123 N. Second St., Stillwater, MN 55082; E-mail: *ttheurer@voyageurpress.com*; *www.publishersroundtable.org*.

Mountains and Plains Booksellers Association, Lisa Knudsen (Executive Director), 19 Old Town Square, Suite 238, Fort Collins, CO 80524; phone (970) 484-5856; (800) 752-0249; e-mail: *info@mountainsplains.org*; *www.mountainsplains.org*.

New Atlantic Independent Booksellers Association, Eileen Dengler (Executive Director), 2667 Hyacinth St., Westbury, NY 11590; phone (877) 866-2422; e-mail: *info@naiba.com*; *www.naiba.com*.

New England Booksellers Association, c/o Wayne "Rusty" Drugan (Executive Director), 1770 Massachusetts Ave. #332, Cambridge, MA 02140; phone (800) 466-8711; e-mail: *rusty@newengland.org*; *www.newenglandbooks.org*.

New Mexico Book Association, 310 Read St., P.O. Box 1285, Santa Fe, NM 87504; phone (505) 983-1412; e-mail: *richard@oceantree.com*; *www.nmbook.org*.

New Orleans-Gulf South Booksellers Association, Joseph Billingsley/ Britton Trice (cochairs), P.O. Box 750043, New Orleans, LA 70175-0043; phone (504) 368-1175, x322; e-mail: *nogsba@yahoo. com*; *www.nogsba.com*.

New York/New Jersey Booksellers Association, Fern Jaffe (President), c/o Paperbacks Plus, 3718 Riverdale Ave., Bronx, NY 10463; phone (718) 796-3119.

Northern California Independent Booksellers Association, Karen Pennington (President), The Presidio, 37 Graham St., P.O. Box 29169, San Francisco, CA 94129; phone (415) 561-7686; e-mail: *office@nciba.com*; *www.nciba.com*.

Oklahoma Independent Booksellers Association, Joanie Stephenson (President), c/o Steve's Sundry, Books & Magazines, 2612 S. Harvard, Tulsa, OK 74114; phone (918) 743-3544; e-mail: *info@stevessundrybooksmags.com*.

Pacific Northwest Booksellers Association, Thom Chambliss (Executive Director), 317 W. Broadway, #214, Eugene, OR 97401- 2890; phone (541) 683-4363; e-mail: *info@pnba.org*; *www.pnba.org*.

San Diego Booksellers Association, Kris Nelson (President-elect), c/o Bluestocking Books; 3817 Fifth Ave., San Diego, CA 92103-3140; phone (619) 296-1424; e-mail: *info@sdbooks.org*; *www.sdbooks.org*.

South Central Booksellers Association, Julia Bentley (President), c/o Memphis State University Bookstore, University Center, Memphis, TN 38152; phone (901) 678-2011.

Southeast Booksellers Association, Wanda Jewell (Executive Director), 1404 S. Beltline Blvd., Columbia, SC 29205; phone (803) 252-7755; e-mail: *info@sebaweb.org*; *www.sebaweb.org*.

Southern California Booksellers Association, Jennifer Bigelow (Executive Director), 301 E. Colorado Blvd., Ste. 501, Pasadena, CA 91101; phone (626) 791-9455; e-mail: *scba@earthlink.net*; *http://scba.bookpage.com*.

Southwestern Booksellers Association, Marvin C. Steakley, (President), c/o Southern Methodist University Bookstore, Box 8362, Dallas, TX 75205-0362.

Upper Midwest Booksellers Association, Susan Walker (Executive Director), 3407 W. 44th St., Minneapolis, MN 55410; phone (800) 784-7522; e-mail: *umbaoffice@aol.com*; *www.abookaday.com*.

PUBLISHING-RELATED TRADE ORGANIZATIONS

Audio Publishers Association, 627 Aviation Way, Manhattan Beach, CA 90266; Tel. (310) 372-0546.

Business Products Industry Association, 301 N. Fairfax Street, Alexandria, VA 22314-2696; Tel. (703) 549-9040; Web site: www.bpia.org.

Calendar Marketing Association, 710 E. Ogden Avenue, Suite 600, Naperville, IL 60563; Tel. (630) 369-2406; Web site: www.calendarmarketplace.com.

Comics Magazine Association of America, 355 Lexington Avenue, New York, NY 10017-6603; Tel. (212) 661-4261.

Electronic Industries Association, 2500 Wilson Blvd., Arlington, VA 22201; Tel. (703) 907-7500; Web site: www.eia.org.

Game Manufacturers Association, Box 602, Swanton, OH 43558; Tel. (419) 826-4262; Web site: www.gama.org.

Gift Association of America, Inc., 608 W. Broad Street, Bethlehem, PA 18018; Tel. (610) 861-9445.

Greeting Card Association, 1200 G Street NW, Suite 760, Washington, DC 20005; Tel. (202) 393-1778; Web site: www.greetingcard.org.

Hobby Industry of America, 319 E. 54th Street, P.O. Box 348, Elmwood Park, NJ 07407; Tel. (201) 794-1133; Web site: www.hobby.org.

International Licensing Industry Merchandisers' Association, 350 Fifth Avenue, Suite 2309, New York, NY 10118; Tel. (212) 244-1944; Web site: www.licensingworld.com/showcase/lima.html.

International Periodical Distributors Association, P.O. Box 3540, Allentown, PA 18106-0540; Tel. (610) 965-3651.

Magazine Publishers of America, 919 Third Avenue, 22nd floor, New York, NY 10022; Tel. (212) 752-0055.

Museum Store Association, 4100 E. Mississipi Avenue, Suite 800, Denver, CO 80246; Tel. (303) 504-9223; Web site: www.museumdistrict.com.

Periodical Wholesalers of North America, 175 Bloor Street E. #1007 S. Tower, Toronto, Ontario M4W 3R8, Canada; Tel. (416) 968-7218.

Recording Industry Association of America, 1330 Connecticut Avenue, Suite 300, Washington, DC 20036; Tel. (202) 775-0101; Web site: *www.riaa.com*.

Software and Information Industry Association, 1730 M Street NW, Suite 700, Washington, DC 20036; Tel. (202) 452-1600; Web site: *www.siia.net*.

Toy Manufacturers of America, Inc., 1115 Broadway, Suite 400, New York, NY 10010; Tel. (212) 675-1141; Web site: *www.toy-tma.com*.

Video Software Dealers Association, 16530 Ventura Blvd., Suite 400, Encino, CA 91436; Tel. (818) 385-1500; Web site: *www.vsda.org*.

Index

Books from Allworth Press

Allworth Press is an imprint of Allworth Communications, Inc. Selected titles are listed below.

The Author's Toolkit: A Step-by-Step Guide to Writing and Publishing Your Book, Revised Edition
by Mary Embree (paperback, 5½ × 8½, 192 pages, $16.95)

Starting Your Career as a Freelance Writer
by Moira Anderson Allen (paperback, 6 × 9, 256 pages, $19.95)

writing.com: Creative Internet Strategies to Advance Your Writing Career, Revised Edition
by Moira Anderson Allen (paperback, 6 × 9, 288 pages, $19.95)

The Complete Guide to Book Publicity
by Jodee Blanco (paperback, 6 × 9, 288 pages, $19.95)

Business and Legal Forms for Authors and Self-Publishers, Revised Edition
by Tad Crawford (paperback with CD-ROM, 8½ × 11, 192 pages, $22.95)

The Writer's Legal Guide: An Author's Guild Desk Reference, Third Edition
by Tad Crawford and Kay Murray (paperback, 6 × 9, 320 pages, $19.95)

Marketing Strategies for Writers
by Michael Sedge (paperback, 6 × 9, 256 pages, $16.95)

How to Write Books That Sell, Revised Edition
by L. Perry Wilbur and Jon Samsel (hardcover, 6 × 9, 224 pages, $19.95)

How to Write Articles That Sell, Revised Edition
by L. Perry Wilbur and Jon Samsel (hardcover, 6 × 9, 224 pages, $19.95)

The Writer's Guide to Corporate Communications
by Mary Moreno (paperback, 6 × 9, 192 pages, $19.95)

Writing for Interactive Media: The Complete Guide
by Jon Samsel and Darryl Wimberley (hardcover, 6 × 9, 320 pages, $19.95)